My Secret S

Vienna, Sophia, Constantinople, Nish, Belgrade, Asia Minor, etc

Man who dined with the Kaiser

Alpha Editions

This edition published in 2024

ISBN : 9789361478055

Design and Setting By
Alpha Editions
www.alphaedis.com
Email - info@alphaedis.com

As per information held with us this book is in Public Domain.
This book is a reproduction of an important historical work. Alpha Editions uses the best technology to reproduce historical work in the same manner it was first published to preserve its original nature. Any marks or number seen are left intentionally to preserve its true form.

Contents

CHAPTER I ....- 1 -
CHAPTER II ....- 4 -
CHAPTER III ....- 14 -
CHAPTER IV ....- 22 -
CHAPTER V ....- 29 -
CHAPTER VI ....- 36 -
CHAPTER VII ....- 43 -
CHAPTER VIII ....- 49 -
CHAPTER IX ....- 56 -
CHAPTER X ....- 63 -
CHAPTER XI ....- 73 -
CHAPTER XII ....- 81 -
CHAPTER XIII ....- 87 -

CHAPTER I

INTRODUCTORY

"Were You Afraid?"—About Myself—War Finds Me in England—The German War-Machine—My Travels—The German Spy System—My Three Journeys—I Become a Workman at Krupp's—I Travel in Chocolate—My Most Important Trip—The Risks—Proofs—My Reception in England.

I am not a spy, that I wish to make abundantly clear; I am a journalist, and I love my profession. Equally well I love adventure and sport, the greatest sport in the world, in which the stake is the player's life.

"Were you ever afraid?" a young and charming English girl recently asked me.

"Afraid!" I replied. "Listen! Imagine yourself with two maps next to your skin, each marked with German submarine bases, military works, and the like. Then you are interrogated by half-a-dozen German Secret Service officers. The least hesitation, the slightest faltering in a reply and, at a motion of the hand two German soldiers take you into an adjoining room, strip you, and—ten minutes later you are dead."

The girl blushed: in my earnestness I had forgotten. Yes! I have been afraid many times; yet, with the gambler's instinct, I have continued the game which, sooner or later, will probably end in a little episode in which the protagonists will be myself and a firing party—somewhere in the enemy country.

I am a citizen of a neutral country. Those in high places whom it concerns know all about me, have seen my passports, examined what remains of my ticket on the Balkan Express with its perforation "18—1—16," and can testify from the chain of documents I possess, from which not a link is missing, that I have actually been where I say I have.

When war broke out I found myself in England, and I immediately saw in the terrible struggle great possibilities for myself. I am twenty-six years of age and speak, besides my native tongue, English, German, French and Flemish. I had lived in England before the war broke out, and have learned to love it second only to my own country. I was anxious to help in the great struggle, and I determined to try and find out as much as I could about the great German War-Machine. For twelve months I have been engaged upon this interesting task, visiting Frankfurt, Hanau, Neuwied, Essen (and other cities in Germany), Vienna, Buda Pesth, Bucharest, Sofia, Constantinople, Brasso,

Rustchouk, Adrianople, Nish, Belgrade, Konia (Asia Minor), etc. Incidentally, I have proved that the German spy system is not so perfect as it is considered by many in this country.

In all I have paid three visits to the enemy countries, each time using the same name, but following a different trade or profession. First I was a workman, and crossed the frontier in shamelessly shabby clothes and with very little impedimenta in the way of luggage. I professed to be a steel-driller, having had a very slight experience in that occupation, obtained for the purpose of my visit. In this guise I penetrated the German Holy of Holies, the famous Krupp factories at Essen. Here for some days I worked, until it was discovered what an execrably bad workman I was. Summary and ignominious dismissal followed, but never did a man take his dismissal less to heart than I. I had gathered some interesting and valuable information, and had seen many remarkable things. This was in March, 1915, although the account was not published until February, 1916, as the Censor prohibited my story appearing in the press, no doubt for very good reasons.

My next journey was to Constantinople as a commercial traveller representing a chocolate firm in a neutral country. On this occasion I interviewed Captain von Hersing, and heard from his own lips the account of his wonderful journey in a German submarine (U51) from Wilhelmshaven to Constantinople. I also obtained a great deal of information which was published at the time. This trip was made in June, 1915.

My third trip was by far the most successful. This I made as a journalist, ostensibly on behalf of a leading neutral paper, but in reality for *The Daily Mail*. It will be readily understood that these journeys required most careful forethought. It sounds so easy on paper, but in point of fact it requires much energy, and most careful and cunning preparation. One mistake, one careless word, and there is suspicion with, in all probability, a fatal result. I began to understand what must be the feelings of a soldier going into battle. When he enlists he thinks of all the dangers in a detached sort of way, and regrets leaving his dear ones behind, but as soon as he is in the thick of the fight he forgets all else but the clash of battle; so it was with me.

On my third journey I knew that at any moment I might be recognised by one of the countless German spies that seem to spring up everywhere. I was, however, determined to see the thing through and, once in the enemy country, my nervousness seemed to vanish.

It must be remembered that no one could undertake such journeys as mine in war-time without the assistance of prominent and influential men abroad, and I desire to make what are very inadequate acknowledgments to many distinguished diplomatists in neutral countries, without whose invaluable help I could not have crossed the border into Austria, or, what is far more important, have returned to England.

I quite anticipated that my adventures would be challenged, for they must seem so extraordinary when read in a country where the German Secret Service is regarded as absolutely infallible. So far from this being the case, I have received letters from all sorts of people congratulating me on my return, and not a word of doubt has been raised in any quarter. I was prepared to meet scepticism with documents that no one could refute.

It has also been a source of great gratification to me to know that my discoveries and the information I have accumulated have been of assistance to the Allies, with whom I am in entire sympathy. I have also had the satisfaction of reading in neutral as well as English newspapers that some of the Kaiser's most trusted and efficient Secret Service Agents have been dismissed and *aides-de-camp* suspended.

I have received at the hands of many distinguished and notable Englishmen nothing but kindness. They have examined my proofs, not with suspicion but with the keenest possible interest, and they have embarrassed me with their congratulations. My invariable reply to these touching tributes has been that I owe to England much; she has given to me many friends and shown me great hospitality, and if anything that I have done can help her in the least degree, I shall always regard myself as a privileged person.

CHAPTER II

VIENNA IN WAR TIME

I Set Out for the Enemy Country—The German Official Mind—Turned Back at the Frontier—Arrival at Vienna—The Kindly Hofrat—Hatred of the English—A Subdued City—Hardships—The Hidden Scourge—The Toll of War—Austria's Terrible Casualties—The Tragic 28th Regiment—"Mr. Wu" in Vienna—Interned Englishmen.

It was during the early days of November, 1915, that I conceived the idea of making another journey to Turkey. From various sources I had heard that the Germans, in conjunction with the Turks, were preparing for their great and much-advertised attack upon Egypt. I determined to find out if they were seriously planning this adventure, or if it were merely "bluff" for political purposes. My arrangements were carefully made, because the whole result of an expedition such as this depends upon the precautions taken at the outset. I first went to a neutral country where, some years previously, I had worked as a journalist. I did not find much difficulty in obtaining from the newspaper with which I had been connected papers and credentials in which it was set forth that I was acting as the special correspondent of that journal.

After careful consideration, I decided upon the shortest route to Turkey, which would take me through Germany, Austria, Roumania, and Bulgaria, and I made my plans accordingly. I failed, however, in my object. At the town of Emmerich, on the German border, I was informed by the officials that my papers were unsatisfactory. At first I was somewhat puzzled, knowing the care that I had taken to procure everything necessary, but I soon discovered what the trouble really was. On my passport my name was spelt with an "i," whereas on my special correspondent's card it was spelt with a "y." I verily believe that the meticulous mind of the German officials would refuse to admit the bearer of a passport in which a comma appeared in place of a colon.

I did my utmost to convince the officers that the mistake was trifling, and that I was a *bona fide* journalist. After much discussion and excited expostulation on my part, I was permitted to travel to Munich; but my papers were taken from me, and I was told that I must apply for them in that city at the Kommandantur.

Convinced that everything was now satisfactorily arranged, I resumed my journey. When we reached Düsseldorf I became aware that my name was being loudly called from the platform. For a moment I was thrilled with a sudden fear that my association with an English newspaper had been discovered and that trouble was brewing; but I quickly recovered myself. When the station-master, a lieutenant, and two soldiers—nothing less than this imposing display of force would satisfy the German official mind—presented themselves at the door of my compartment, I confessed to my identity, and was promptly told that I must leave the train, and furthermore, that I should not be allowed to proceed upon my journey until my papers were perfectly in order. The upshot of this incident was that I was forced to return to the frontier, all on account of a careless consulate clerk using an "i" for a "y."

I considered it far too risky to have the correction made and start again. I had acquired some knowledge of German official psychology. Knowing that the Austrian authorities are less difficult than the German, I decided to return to England and journey through France and Switzerland into Austria. In Switzerland I obtained a new passport, and was soon on my way to the Austrian frontier.

On the journey I had some unpleasant meditations. The Austrian authorities might have been informed of my unsuccessful endeavour to cross the German border, and as some eight months previously I had already entered Austria by that same route I now proposed to take, I found myself hesitating as to the advisability of continuing the adventure. "Perhaps," I argued with myself, "it would be advisable to return to safety." I soon, however, overcame this trepidation by the simple process of telling myself that hundreds of thousands of men in the trenches were facing what I should soon be facing—death. I was a soldier, I told myself, as indeed I am holding a commission in my own country as a Reserve officer. Finally, by the time I reached Feldkirch, I was prepared to face the Austrian officials with a stout heart and a grim determination to get through at all costs.

With my fellow travellers I was conducted to a large hall where soldiers, with fixed bayonets, were on guard. To understand my feelings as I stood there awaiting my turn to be taken before the officers for interrogation, one must have been in a similar position oneself.

One by one my companions were admitted to the adjoining room, and when at last my own turn came, I found myself confronting five Austrian officers, all of whom seemed to have developed that inquisitive state of mind which seems to exist only in war-time. In Switzerland I had obtained from the Austrian Ambassador, Baron Gayer, a *laissez passer*, which was of the greatest possible value to me. After an unpleasant ten minutes I found that I had passed with honours, having not only satisfied the officers' demands for information, but earned their goodwill to the extent of being wished good luck and a pleasant journey. An hour later the train left for Vienna, twenty-four hours distant, through the beautiful Austrian Tyrol. I was, however, too tired and travel-weary to be much concerned with the beauties of nature. There was no sleeping accommodation upon the train, and what rest I had was snatched sitting in an upright position.

On the evening of December 8th, 1915, I arrived in Vienna, where I decided to stay at the Park Hotel in preference to one of the more fashionable hotels in the gayer part of the city. I did this with a deliberate purpose, as the Park Hotel is situated close to the two railway stations, Sud Bahnhof and Ost Bahnhof. From my point of vantage I hoped to be able to watch the movements of troops marching to the stations.

I planned to stay only a short time in Vienna, my real objective being Turkey, but I particularly wanted to see Belgrade, which possessed for me a great interest on account of the recent desperate fighting that had taken place there. I had secured an introduction to a distinguished official in the Austrian Foreign Office (Ministerium des Aussern) upon whom it was my first object to call. This important personage, a Hofrat (the German equivalent, I believe, of the English Privy Councillor), received me courteously, and without that suspicion that seems to be the inevitable attribute of the German, listened to my explanation as to the object of my journey, and very kindly promising me all the facilities that he had it in his power to grant.

He gave me an introduction to the War Office (K.U.K. Kriegsministerium) Press Bureau. His letter stated that I was well known to the Foreign Office, and that all possible facilities should be granted to me on my journey to the Near East. This letter eventually produced a document which was of the utmost assistance to me in my subsequent journeyings, and which I still have in my possession.

As he handed to me the introduction to the Kriegsministerium Pressbureau, which was to prove for me my open sesame into Turkey, he remarked: "I am always very careful of giving introductions to the War Office; you yourself, for instance, might be the biggest spy (grosze spion) in the world." I smiled inwardly as I thanked him for his kindness, and congratulated myself that I had been so fortunate as to impress favourably a man who possessed so much authority. When I asked him to furnish me with a passport, enabling me to travel through to Belgrade, he replied that it was not in his power to do so, but that he would do what he could to assist me, and that I should hear from him in due course.

In the meantime I determined to look about the city to discover what changes had taken place during the eight months that had elapsed since my previous visit. The first thing I noticed was the increased hostility on the part of the Viennese towards the English. For this there were two very obvious reasons:

first, the pinch of hunger, "stomach pressure" as it has been called, the work of the British Navy; second, the intervention of Italy, the work of British diplomatists. The Austrian is not so dramatic in his hatreds as the German; but there is a bitter and burning feeling in his heart against a nation that has robbed him of most of the luxuries and many of the necessaries of life, and, in addition, has precipitated him into another war at a time when his hands were already over full.

Unlike London, Paris, and Constantinople, Vienna is brightly lit at night; but the atmosphere of gaiety of this gayest of cities no longer exists. Now it is dull; cafés, which in peace time remained open all night, are forced to close at 11 p.m.; some, but very few, have obtained permission to remain open until midnight. There in Vienna, as everywhere else in the Teutonic war zone, the all-absorbing topic of conversation was the question of food-supply.

There is a humorous side to the situation; humorous, that is, to the Allies. The people of Turkey confidently anticipate obtaining supplies from the Central Powers; whereas the Central Powers are equally optimistic about Turkey's ability to supply them with foodstuffs. The Berlin Press is responsible for the Teutonic error, on account of its bombastic articles on the advantage of opening up Turkey and Asia Minor with their vast resources. For one thing this was to produce butter for Berlin. In Vienna they do not grumble so much as in Berlin about the shortage of butter; but they bitterly resent the absence of cream. One of the chief delights of the city is the famous Vienna coffee, with its foaming crest of whipped cream extending half way down the glass. During my previous visit this had been easily obtainable, but eight months of war had resulted in the prohibition of the sale of milk and cream save for infants, all the rest being used in the manufacture of explosives. When I learned that I should be forced to drink black coffee, I felt a momentary grievance against the Allies.

Of the 1,600 taxis that in peace time whirled gay parties about Vienna, only forty remained, and these are extremely shabby, their tyres having a very decrepit appearance. With the exception of these forty taxis all vehicular traffic stops at 11 p.m., and the Viennese ladies, famed for embonpoint, will long remember the war if only for the amount of walking that they have had to do.

There is also a great scarcity of petrol, tyres, and glycerine, all having been requisitioned by the Government. Lard and other fatty substances used in the preparation of food are of a very inferior quality. I have good cause to remember this as, for four days, I was extremely ill on account of the odious stuff used in the cooking of some food I had eaten.

Curiously enough, I found the bread of a much better quality than during my previous visit; but there was very little of it, for the reign of the bread-ticket was not yet over. Meat was scarce and very expensive. As a rule, I dined at the Restaurant Hartmann, in peace time a well-known place for good dinners. I found, however, that it had greatly deteriorated, that the food was far from good and ridiculously expensive. For a meal consisting of soup, meat and vegetables, with some fruit, I had to pay eight kronen (a kronen being 10d.), double the peace price. Some idea of the scarcity of meat may be obtained from the fact that a single portion of roast beef costs about four kronen (3s. 4d.). I should explain that Hartmann's is not a place like the Ritz Hotel, but a middle-class restaurant where in time of peace the prices are extremely moderate.

That terrible scourge, which seems to follow in the footsteps of civilisation, has increased alarmingly in Vienna since the outbreak of war. Soldiers go to the vilest part of the city deliberately inviting contagion so that they may not be sent to the front. The eyes of the military authorities have been opened to the seriousness of the situation, and the men are very seriously punished.

A VIENNA BREAD-TICKET

Vienna is full of wounded; in fact, I have never seen a city in which there were so many. I tried to find out as much as I could about the number of Austrian wounded throughout the country, but it was extremely difficult to glean information. In order that the public shall not be unduly depressed, the wounded are carefully scattered about in different towns and villages, particularly in Bohemia. Germans have told me that they have heard the same thing in regard to England, where hundreds of little Red Cross hospitals were to be found in provincial towns and villages all over the country!

The German method is also to keep the wounded away from the big towns as much as possible. The smaller villages are used for Red Cross stations. When in Frankfurt on one of my former trips I one day remarked to an old woman, a farmer's wife with whom I got into conversation, that I could not understand why there were so few wounded in a large town such as Frankfurt. "Come and have a look at our village," she answered, "we have them in our houses." I accordingly went to Andernach, which was the name of the village. She gave me coffee and war bread, and treated me very kindly. There were six wounded soldiers in her house, and I learned that there was hardly a village on the slopes of the Rhine where wounded soldiers were not billeted to benefit by the invigorating air of the Rhineland hills, having first been treated in the hospitals. I was told by one of the wounded soldiers that in a hospital about half-an-hour's run from Cologne 180 soldiers were lying disabled.

The Austrian authorities have their own particular methods; they arrange, for instance, that only a third of the convalescent soldiers shall be allowed out at the same time. Thus, if there are three hundred wounded in a hospital who are able to walk, only one hundred are permitted out at the same time for fresh air and exercise.

The number of blind soldiers is amazing. It was one of the most terrible sights I saw. Before Italy participated in the war the total number of Austrian soldiers who had lost their sight was 10,000, now it is 80,000. I was informed of this by Dr. Robert Otto Steiner, the head of the largest hospital in Vienna, probably the largest in the world, the Wiener Allgemeines Krankenhaus, which has 8,000 beds, and 3,000 being occupied by men who have lost their sight.

The reason for this terrible number of blind soldiers is that in the mountains the troops cannot dig adequate trenches, and the Italian shells burst against the mountains and send showers of rock-fragments in all directions. It was with a mournful expression that Dr. Steiner told me of the 70,000 Austrians blinded within six months. I asked him what was to happen to these poor fellows after the war, and he confessed that they presented a problem which seemed beyond the power of any Government to solve. Whether or not a monument be erected to the Kaiser in the Sieges-Allée, there will be throughout Europe thousands of living monuments to his "greatness" in the shape of the blind, the mad, and the paralysed, who will breathe curses upon the name German Militarism that has robbed them of nearly all save life itself.

In the course of my wanderings about the city I heard an amusing story about recruiting in England. It was told me by some Austrian officers, who were convinced that recruiting in this country had been a success. Their explanation was that the aristocracy had obtained from the Government an assurance that they would be retained for home service, whereas the poor would be sent to the front. Nothing that I heard showed a greater ignorance of the sporting instinct of the English gentleman than this grotesque statement, and that in spite of the ubiquitous Wolff and his wireless war news. Speaking of Wolff reminds me of a saying among the supporters of the Allies in Constantinople which runs: "There are lies, there are damned lies, and there are Wolff's wireless messages."

One night I had an interesting conversation with a captain in the Austrian Polish Legion, whose name is in my possession, but which in his own interest I refrain from printing. He told me several things which showed clearly the difficulties which the Germans are experiencing in combining their vastly varied forces. "I am with the Austrians now," he said, "fighting the Russians because of the comparatively good treatment we Poles received from Austria. After the war we are promised a Polish Republic. If, however," he added, "it comes to fighting for Prussia against the Russians, I for one shall desert and join Russia."

It has been known in this country for some months that something had gone wrong with regard to the Austrian 28th Regiment of the line, the Prague Regiment, which consists entirely of Bohemians principally drawn from Prague, who being Slavs hate the Germans. From this officer I heard the story of the tragic 28th. In the National Museum in Vienna there are several flags draped in black—they are those of this ill-fated regiment of Bohemians.

It was the intention of the whole of the regiment to desert to the Russians, the plot including officers as well as rank and file. One day, seeing before them what they took to be Russian regiments, the soldiers threw down their arms and held up their hands in token of surrender. But the "Russians" were Prussians! The Bohemians were unaware that the round cap of Russia is practically the same as that worn in the Prussian armies. The Prussian officers immediately grasped the situation, and turned machine-guns on the defenceless men, massacring hundreds of them. The remainder were taken prisoners, and eventually one out of every five was shot, and of the officers one in every three was executed. The men who remained were sent to the most dangerous part of the front, and there are now very few left to tell the terrible story. The flags in the National Museum are a record of the disgrace of a regiment whose name no longer appears in the Austrian Army List.

One thing that struck me in particular was that the most popular play in Vienna should be the English success, "Mr. Wu." It was advertised all over the city, beneath the title in smaller letters appearing the words "Der Mandarin." The original title being in heavy letters, whilst the German title is added in smaller type, it being evidently considered that the words "Mr. Wu" required some explanation for Austrian eyes. I was at a loss to account for this anomaly. I remembered having seen the play several times in London, but this did not supply any information as to its popularity in an enemy city.

One evening I went to the Neues Wiener Stadttheater, a handsome building erected since the outbreak of war. The audience was mostly composed of women, less than a fourth being men. The play was admirably staged, but I missed Matheson Lang. I soon discovered the reason for its popularity. An English business man is shown to great disadvantage beside a Chinaman, and this seemed greatly to please the audience. At the end of every act the curtain was raised time after time and the performers loudly applauded.

To me the real tragedy of Vienna is that of the Englishmen of military age who cannot leave the city. They are well-treated and allowed their liberty so long as they do not leave the city, which shows how much milder is the Austrian as compared with the German rule. They are, however, expected to be within doors by 8 o'clock at night. Notices have appeared in the papers to the effect that subjects of belligerent countries are to be freely allowed to use their own language in public places as long as they do so in a way that is not offensive. The poor fellows are hungry for news. The last English paper they had seen was *The Times* of September 3rd. They speak feelingly of the hated war bread, but they admit the great improvement in its quality during the last two months. They spoke well of the Austrian treatment, but for all this their position is far from enviable. They are in the midst of a hostile population, knowing nothing of what is actually happening to their country, and eager to be in the trenches beside their fellow countrymen.

There was much talk about the Baghdad and Egyptian campaigns, and also about the depreciation in the value of the kroner, the Austrian standard coin, which is now worth only half its original value. Far-seeing men among the Viennese regard this as significant.

Great precautions are taken with regard to people arriving in Vienna from Hungary. For some time past cholera and the Plague have been raging in some parts of that country, although very little information leaks out on account of the severity of the censorship. Occasionally, however, news comes through that proves the situation to be far from favourable. For months previously Hungary was the scene of the great concentration of the

German and Austrian armies for the fighting in the Balkans. The massing of these troops in a comparatively small area inevitably results in the spread of disease.

CHAPTER III

IN THE BALKANS

I Leave Vienna—Gay Bucharest—The Bandmaster's Indiscretion—"*À bas les allemands!*"—Roumania Eager for War—German Devices—An English Cigarette—A Terrible Journey—The Spoils of War—The Wily German—Bulgarian Poverty Under the Germans—Austrian Satisfaction over the Serbian Victories—Compulsion in England—Bulgarian Anxiety about the Attitude of Greece—The German Language in Bulgaria.

At the end of about a fortnight I left Vienna, having received my passport. I had become convinced of the uselessness of endeavouring to travel over Serbia to Turkey, and therefore decided to go round by way of Roumania. As a matter of fact, this was the only course open to me. By way of Buda Pesth, where the Austrian State Railway ends, and that of Hungary begins, I went to Brasso, the last station on Hungarian territory. On my previous journey the frontier station had been Pre-deal, but this being on Roumanian territory the Austrians found that they had no power to act in the event of catching spies, consequently they removed to Brasso. I arrived at Brasso at 5 a.m., after a thirty hours' journey. As the train for Bucharest did not leave until noon, I had time to look round the delightful little town, nestling among the Carpathian mountains.

Although small, Brasso is of considerable importance at the present moment, owing to its being the headquarters of the Austrian army destined to act against Roumania should difficulties arise. The place was full of soldiers, foot, horse and artillery, with guns of every kind and calibre. The civil population seemed to have disappeared entirely. On the surrounding mountains military manœuvres were everywhere in operation. I was told that there were 80,000 troops concentrated at Brasso.

It was at Brasso railway station that I first discovered the great value of the War Office passport I had obtained in Vienna. Without looking at my luggage, and scarcely glancing at my papers, the officials allowed me to pass, and I blessed my good friend the Hofrat. A more miserable journey I have never experienced than that to Bucharest. All the blinds in the carriages were lowered as a military precaution, although Roumania is not at war. This circumstance, however, testifies to the precautions being taken by the Roumanians against the invasion of their territory. A Roumanian gentleman travelling in the same carriage assured me that everywhere trenches and field-works were in course of construction.

The difference between Vienna and Bucharest, "Little Paris," as it is called, where I arrived at seven in the evening, is most striking. The Roumanian capital, always noted for its gaiety, is the Mecca of pleasure lovers, and so far from the war having diminished this spirit it seems greatly to have increased it. The population has been considerably augmented, money is spent and wasted everywhere, cafés and theatres do a thriving trade, and the number of motor cars and pair-horse carriages is astonishing considering the smallness of the city. Now that the export of wheat from Russia to the Central Empires is no longer possible, Roumania has become the wheat market of the Balkans. I was told that the third crop of the year had just been harvested, and every quarter of cereals that can be produced is readily sold. The result is that money flows everywhere like water.

I look back upon my stay in Bucharest as an oasis of peace in a desert of danger. The Roumanians are a delightful people, and the Allies should appreciate how much they owe to the strictly neutral attitude of Roumania in regard to the war. The Roumanian Government prevented food, coal, or other necessities from reaching either Austria or Turkey. Owing to the new Balkan Express, the Roumanian preventive measures do not now possess its former significance.

The Bulgarian attitude towards the Entente Powers was always a little difficult to determine; the mass of the Bulgarian people is by no means cordial to either Germany or Turkey. The politicians most likely became nervous, and German gold did the rest. Nevertheless, I failed to find any evidence of Bulgarian affection for Great Britain. The people in general know hardly anything about this country. There is a vague remembrance of Gladstone in the minds of the better-educated. About Germany, however, every Bulgarian knows, thanks to the indefatigable newspaper work, the German schools, the ubiquitous German kinematograph exhibition, and the "peaceful penetration" by German bagmen, German music, and other elements of German Kultur propaganda.

Little Roumania occupies an extraordinary position in the war. Surrounded by the warring nations, she herself is at peace. There is no doubt as to her friendly feelings towards the Quadruple Entente.

In Bucharest I stayed at the Hotel Frascati, where I spent four delightful days entirely free from all anxiety. It was on the second day of my visit that I received the first evidence of Roumania's attitude. In the evening I went to the Casino de Paris, where the audience formed quite a cosmopolitan crowd. When the band played the *Marseillaise* a party of Germans, who had evidently been dining well rather than judiciously, expressed their feelings by whistling loudly and making other noises. The audience, however, loudly applauded the band, and the incident terminated.

Shortly afterwards one of the thick-skinned Teutons offered the bandmaster a 20 mark note (£1) to play *Die Wacht am Rhein*. The bandmaster was willing to take the 20 marks, but expressed some doubt as to whether the musicians would play the required air. Furthermore he expressed himself as very doubtful as to the effect of the melody upon the people assembled in the Casino. He eventually overcame alike the compunction of his band and his own misgivings, but the orchestra had hardly started before pandemonium broke out. "*À bas les Allemands!*" and other cries were shouted on every side, with an occasional "*À bas les bosches!*" and the band came to a sudden stop. The Germans left the Casino in some haste, to the accompaniment of the hisses of the audience.

Roumania is all for the Entente Powers, and in particular she is pro-French. Her especial hatred is for Austria, and in a superlative degree for Hungary. One evening I went to a kinematograph exhibition entitled "Under the Yoke of Austria-Hungary," which depicted the sufferings of Roumanians living under Austrian rule. At one particular incident the audience rose to their feet and shrieked "Down with Austria! Down with Hungary!" These demonstrations are by no means rare, and they show very clearly the general trend of Roumanian public opinion.

The whole Roumanian army is eager for war. I reveal no secret in stating this, for Roumania is overrun with German spies. During my short stay I came in contact with many Roumanian officers, who expressed themselves as very dissatisfied with the slowness of the Entente operations. They are, however, firm believers in the eventual victory of the Allies, and they assured me that no influence, no pressure, political or otherwise, could induce them to join with Germany. They do not appreciate quite all the difficulties with which the Allies have to deal. Germany has been preparing for this war for more than a generation; the Triple Entente Powers were taken by surprise and have been greatly handicapped. This I strove to point out to my Roumanian acquaintances, urging them to "wait and see."

I hesitate to offer advice to the British Government; but I wish in the interests of itself and its Allies that it could be persuaded as to the necessity— no milder word is suitable—of making known in Roumania the magnificent work of the British Army and Navy. The instinctive sympathy of the Roumanians is with the French and Italians; for it must be remembered that they are a Latin people. Their newspapers publish a great deal about the French and Italian armies. The Germans have their own newspapers, printed in the Roumanian tongue. German propaganda and German gold are to be encountered everywhere, the chief object being to keep Roumania neutral.

A favourite device with the Germans is to exaggerate every mishap to the Allies, magnify every success of their own into a great victory, and above all to point out to Roumania the magnitude of the task that the Entente Powers have undertaken. When I was in Bucharest the chief theme of the German newspapers was the Dardanelles. Long accounts of English defeats appeared in their journals, all lavishly illustrated. The Roumanian is not devoid of intelligence, and he can fairly well appraise Prussian character, and he would rather fight to the last man than share the fate of Belgium, Serbia, or Montenegro; still he cannot be entirely indifferent to the clever German propaganda.

From the plenty, the music, and the white bread of Bucharest I set out for Sofia. At Giugiu, the Roumanian frontier-station on the Danube, I took the ferry across to Rustchouk, in Bulgarian territory. Here I had to spend a day and night waiting for the train. Rustchouk is a terrible little place, ankle-deep in mud, and I looked forward with dismay to the dreary hours I should have to spend in this awful hole. But all things have their compensations, and I was able to glean some very interesting information.

On the Danube I noticed four Austrian monitors, which were there, I was told, to protect the Austrian and Bulgarian cities on the river bank against Russian attack. I also noticed with the keenest interest huge quantities of light railway material, mostly rails and sleepers, which were being brought down by boat and landed at the Bulgarian port on their way to Turkey. All this material, I was told, is destined for the campaign against Egypt.

I found the Bulgarian authorities much more difficult than the Austrian; this I remembered from my previous trip, and I had taken the precaution of obtaining a special passport at the Bulgarian Legation in Vienna. Even with this invaluable document in my possession I experienced considerable difficulty, and was subjected to much questioning before I was allowed to pass. These unpleasant and nerve-racking interrogations were dreadful ordeals, to which I never seemed to be able to accustom myself. Perhaps I was too imaginative, but the consequences of a possible slip were always before me.

During my first visit to Vienna in war time I had a very unpleasant experience, showing the necessity for constant care. One day I encountered in the streets of Vienna a young Englishman I had known in London, who had not been interned. He gave me a cigarette, and subsequently came to my hotel. I was promptly challenged for smoking an English cigarette, which, coupled with the fact that I had some acquaintance with an Englishman, resulted in my arrest, and I spent an unpleasant day in an Austrian prison. This little incident, which involved endless mental strain, shows how necessary it was for me to be for ever watchful. It must be remembered that my journey occupied some seven weeks.

As I slopped through the abominably muddy streets of Rustchouk, I noticed German soldiers and non-commissioned officers everywhere; they seemed to be in charge of everything, including the port works and all the military buildings. I discovered that there was a serious shortage of sugar, and I had to drink my tea and coffee without it. Milk likewise was unobtainable, and if there is one thing in life above all others that is necessary to me it is milk and cream. Some one once told me that I must have been intended for a kitten.

I was obliged to stay in a very dirty hotel that rejoiced in the name of the Hotel Bristol, where the available accommodation was of the most primitive description. The bed was so dirty that I gave it up as a bad job, and slept in two arm-chairs. The next day I left for Sofia, a journey which occupied twenty hours, largely owing to the shortage of coal. I have never had a more monotonous train journey. The windows were painted white, as the suspicious Bulgars are determined that no one shall learn any military secrets by looking out of the train. Imagine the monotony of sitting for twenty hours in a small compartment without a chance of glancing out at the countryside. I had no newspapers, no cigarettes, and no food. Nothing but the opposite side of the carriage at which to gaze, or the whited panes of glass with which to occupy myself, for nearly a day and a night. I passed most of the time by sleeping in fitful snatches.

At every little station where the train stopped I got out and endeavoured to purchase food. At one place, to my great joy, I succeeded in obtaining some stale bread and a piece of chocolate of obviously pre-war manufacture. I did not dare to drink water for fear of cholera, and when I eventually arrived in Sofia I was in a state of collapse and was thankful to get to the "Splendid" Hotel, which lies in the heart of the city.

There was none of the gaiety of Bucharest about Sofia. For four days I had forgotten war, but here it was brought once more vividly to my mind. Swaggering German officers were everywhere; for the German occupation is firmly established, and nearly as complete as at Constantinople. There seemed to be no social life, dulness reigning supreme, and I longed for the brightness and plenty of Bucharest. Curiously enough, the most striking thing about Sofia is the Turkish Baths, which have their place in a wonderful new building; they are considered the finest Turkish Baths in the world.

It was in Sofia that I heard another instance of German thoroughness and subtilty. When, through the medium of Turkey the Germans were bribing Arab chiefs to fight against the British, the gifts consisted not only of money, jewellery and horses, but of Circassian beauties from the Turkish harems. I had not the pleasure of seeing these ladies who had the honour of cementing international alliances. In dealing with the Bulgar the German is equally wily, and magnanimously hands over to him all the tragic booty dragged from the poor Serbian homes. Guns, munitions, rifles, household furniture and jewellery, and loot of every possible description, from little Serbia, was to be found everywhere in Sofia.

Nor has this system of bribery been without its marked effect, for I saw everywhere German and Bulgarian officers mixing together and having a good time, and a good deal of sweethearting was going on between German soldiers and Bulgarian girls.

In Sofia only black bread is obtainable. Sugar was absolutely unprocurable, coal was short, but prices were not so high as in Constantinople. The Bulgarian people, however, are suffering the lot which seems to follow inevitably in the wake of the German wherever he goes—shortage of food and other supplies.

I wish that I could have had with me one or two British Cabinet Ministers; not that they might suffer any harm, or endanger their valuable lives, but that they might have learned to appreciate the value of the weapon which they have not yet learned how to use—the British Navy. One of the most certain ways of shortening the war is to bring about dissensions, not only in Germany, but among the population of her subjugated allies—Austria-Hungary, Bulgaria and Turkey—and this can best be done by what the Germans call "Stomach Pressure."

There seems to be still a small amount of silver in circulation in Sofia, but the Bulgars, who have always been poor, are now realising an unprecedented degree of poverty under their German masters. If properly emphasised this must, in my opinion, bring about eventual trouble with the Prussian Bully, who is at present cajoling them with gifts, but principally with promises.

The conquest of Serbia has unquestionably greatly heartened the Austrians, who are more anti-Serbian than anti-Russian. Since the war broke out there have been periods when the Berlin taskmasters found themselves in some difficulty as to how to maintain the enthusiasm of their Austrian allies. Upon this I am absolutely convinced, there is no such difficulty now. It is so many years since unhappy Austria has had cause to celebrate a victory that the novelty of the sensation has had a remarkably stimulating effect upon the whole country. Their history has been a story of retreat and defeat. Prussia crushed them in a few weeks in 1866, now they begin to regard themselves as the equals of their overlords. In addition to their new port of Antivari on the Adriatic, they confidently anticipate securing Venice and Northern Serbia. For the moment they are intoxicated with victory which they fondly imagine to be their own, but underneath there is the same hatred of the Prussian that existed before the war.

The compulsion campaign in England has aroused great interest in Austria, and has been the cause of innumerable heated arguments in the thousands of cafés throughout the land. The popular idea that Englishmen fight only when they are paid to do so, with extra for battles, has been so assiduously fostered by Berlin propagandists that it has become almost an article of Austrian faith. It is practically impossible for them to understand the spirit of the new British armies, to which men have flocked from all parts of the Empire. In Vienna, as in other places, I was solemnly assured that the rich would stay at home and play football, or live in their castles, hunting and enjoying themselves. Not even eighteen months of war have dispelled the Austrian belief in English "sportkrankheit" (sport disease).

The day after I arrived in Sofia, I had an interesting talk with two Bulgarian officers who were staying in the same hotel. They told me of the retreat of the Franco-British forces from Serbian territory into Greece. The Bulgarian soldiers liked very much to fight the English, for the reason that when they defeated them the booty they find is so considerable. For instance, many of those Bulgarian farmers had never seen or eaten chocolate in their lives, and were delighted to find, when the English had to evacuate the camp, that they left behind them considerable quantities of chocolate and marmalade.

In particular, these Bulgarian officers were keen to know something of the situation in Greece. As I came from a foreign country they thought I should be able to tell them much about what Greece was going to do. After talking with them for a little while I got the impression that they seemed to fear the participation of Greece in the war. They do not like the Greeks; in fact, they hate them. There have always been quarrels between these two countries; but, at the same time, these Bulgarians were not particularly keen to fight the Greeks just then. When I asked the reason why, they told me that a great part of the army had to be ready for eventualities against Roumania and Russia, and that the rest would not be sufficient to meet the Grecian army with any chance of success, reinforced as it could be by a large Franco-British army. I thought to myself, if only the leading Greek statesmen with their pro-German king could hear this, what a fine opportunity it would be for Greece to settle her old quarrels with Bulgaria.

One thing struck me very much, that wherever the Germans go a shortage of food and other things seems to follow on their heels. When I had visited Bulgaria eight months previously, there was not what one would call an abundance of food, but there was enough to keep people going. As soon as the Germans got the Bulgarians to march with them the scarcity of food began. The first Sugar Ticket had just been issued when I entered Bulgaria, and I dare say other tickets will soon follow. People, particularly women, were worrying the officials as to where these tickets were available, and shouts of all kinds showed abundantly that the people were very little pleased with the new regulations. The financial situation as well seems to be hopeless. There is paper money everywhere. Of silver there is very little, and gold of course is unknown.

It is a remarkable thing that of all the Balkan countries Bulgaria is the only one where the German language is known to any extent. They call themselves proudly "Little Germany," but to the honour of the Bulgarians I must say there is a marked difference between the Bulgarian and the German. He is not brutal, very simple, and extremely polite, three things of which no German can be accused. The officers go about with the soldiers in the same way as the French. They are very simple and unassuming. I saw in the train a Bulgarian captain produce from his pocket a piece of sausage and start eating it sitting before us, a thing a German officer would never do.

In most schools previous to the war French was the first language taught; now they all start with German. All the same, fifty per cent. of the Bulgarian officers I saw and spoke with completely ignored the German language, and the only language in which we could make each other understood was French.

CHAPTER IV

CONSTANTINOPLE

I Leave Sofia—A Valuable Document—The Change in Adrianople—The Bulgars in Possession—The Turk Determined to Fight—I Adopt the Fez—War Pressure—The Fate of Enemy Subjects—A Way They Have in Turkey—The Financial Situation—Enver Goes to Berlin—A Turkish Girl Clerk—A Quick Change—A City of Darkness.

I stayed only a few days in Sofia, and soon continued my journey to Constantinople. The train left about two in the morning, but as we were told on the afternoon previous that the train would leave at 11 p.m. that night, we, my fellow passengers and I, were all there at the railway station at 10 o'clock, and had to wait four hours in a nasty, dirty-looking waiting room, filled with German soldiers and Bulgarian soldiers and officers. It was uncomfortably warm in the room. Most of the Germans were playing cards, and I was longing to get out into the fresh air, but no one was allowed on to the platform.

My *laissez passer* from the Bulgarian Minister at Vienna again proved invaluable, and I found out to my great satisfaction that this paper would serve me in many ways. As soon as I showed it to the Bulgarian Commandant I was allowed on the platform. There I found myself, the special correspondent of an English newspaper, allowed more privileges than even German civil travellers—a thing that made me smile. Most of the German soldiers were on the way to Constantinople and Asia Minor, and some of them told me that they had not seen their homes since the beginning of the war. They were not complaining, however, as they seemed to be convinced that the victory would be theirs. They were well-clothed, and looked well-fed also, and I did not notice any old Landsturm men. We in this country are too often inclined to believe that the German man supply is exhausted. The men they send to the Balkans, however, have by no means the appearance of being the last of the bunch; in fact, no one could wish for better soldiers, every one of them being of excellent physique.

When I eventually left Sofia I was faced with a journey of twenty-four hours, once more with carriage windows painted white; but this time I had the good fortune to secure sleeping-car accommodation, and I promptly turned in; there was nothing else to do. We were four in a sleeping-car compartment. The man opposite to me was a German merchant on his way to Asia Minor to buy wool, which, as is well known, is one of the great products of Turkey. He seemed very tired, and did not respond at all well to my efforts to engage him in conversation. Soon he was snoring with such earnestness that I had considerable difficulty in getting to sleep myself.

The next morning we arrived at Adrianople. What a change from the Adrianople I had seen eight months before! There were no Turkish soldiers, no Turkish flags, no Turkish lettering at the station. Bulgarian soldiers were guarding the line, Bulgarian flags were flying from the railway station, and Bulgarian letters indicated the name of the place.

During the last few years the Holy City of the Turks has experienced many vicissitudes. In the first Balkan War it was captured by the Bulgars, aided by the Serbs. When difficulties arose between the various members of the Balkan League, owing to the treacherous conduct of Bulgaria, the Turks retook the town, but their reign was short, and now they have surrendered it once more to the Bulgars. There was not a single Turkish soldier to be seen at the railway station, and, to add to the irony of the situation, the Turks have almost completed a fine new railway station, which I suppose the Bulgars will presently take over, allowing a minimum sum as compensation.

As soon as my train drew up at Adrianople, German soldiers rushed into the different carriages to ask for German newspapers. While I was in Constantinople I found that the only paper printed in English that was allowed to be sold was *The Continental Times*, a German propagandist journal with a very obvious purpose.

It should interest English readers to know that everywhere the Turks regard themselves as fighting for their very existence. Such being the case, the Allies must not deceive themselves as to the desperate character of the resistance which the Turks will continue to offer. All are convinced that war with the Allies was inevitable, for the reason that Constantinople had been promised to Russia. A Turkish deputy "friend" of mine was never tired of harping on this note.

At Lule Burgas there were further interrogations, and once more I had to go through the ordeal of cross-examination, but thanks to the personal letter I carried from the Turkish Ambassador in Vienna to Halil Bey, the Turkish Minister for Foreign Affairs, my difficulties were soon over. In fact, the officials were very polite, and wished me a good journey.

Not only has Adrianople become merged in Bulgarian territory, but Lule Burgas, the station beyond, has also passed into the possession of the Bulgars. It was not until I was past Lule Burgas that I met the first Turkish soldiers.

The impression I got of Turkey in Europe was that of a poor and monotonous country; nowhere did I discover anyone cultivating the soil, and, with the exception of the miserable little villages that we passed, it was quite possible to imagine oneself in an uninhabited country.

It was one o'clock in the morning when I reached Stamboul, the Turkish part of Constantinople. I went direct to the Pera Palace Hotel, being conveyed in an old carriage, the only one I found available. Not a light of any description was to be seen, the town being in utter darkness. The Pera Palace Hotel is well known to many Englishmen as being the only good hotel in the place. It is now more than ever expensive, prices having been greatly increased. I could live cheaper at the Ritz Hotel in London than in the Pera Palace Hotel in Constantinople. After a few hours' sleep, I set out upon an exploration of the city, which I knew from my previous visit. What a change!

My first precaution was to adopt the fez as a head covering. When in Rome do as Rome does, is an excellent maxim, more particularly so in war time. Over and over again I had noticed that some sort of uniform is the best means of facilitating travel in a country occupied by soldiery. In Constantinople the fez is almost an introduction. But of the changes I noticed: bad food, bread-tickets, or rather bread-books, the bread itself practically uneatable, the hotel swarming with German officers grumbling bitterly at the fare, and all talking bombastically of Egypt.

In Constantinople one realises the war pressure better than in any other of the great capitals in the war zone that I have visited. The dearth of the necessaries of life has become alarming. None the less the Germans who swarm the streets, the Government offices, and the railway trains see to it that they themselves are well fed and well provided with every requisite. The more I saw of the German side of the war, the more I realised that the care and attention of the entire German people is being concentrated on the Army, that, while all the other Government offices in Constantinople were shabby, as they have always been, while electric light and gas light exist no longer, the German-controlled War Office had been entirely redecorated inside and out, and looks as spick and span as if it were in reality Prussian.

The defenceless subjects of the nations at present fighting the Turks who are still in Constantinople have to suffer many indignities. It is disheartening to describe. To my great satisfaction I found that nearly all the English colony had left before hostilities broke out, but many French and Belgians remained, also a number of Russians, who for some reason or other stayed behind. They are in a deplorable condition. Many of these people before the war belonged to the wealthy classes, but at present they are poor and dependent. One Belgian with whom I had become acquainted on my first visit, a very reliable and honest business man, told me many interesting things.

When war broke out he was living with his wife and three children on the Asia Minor coast, the other side of the Bosphorus, which must be considered a suburb of Constantinople. Nearly every business man has only his office in Constantinople, ninety per cent. of them living on the Asia Minor coast, which is far more healthy, clean, and agreeable. This Belgian possessed, besides the house in which he was living, four other houses, and a farm some 20 miles inland. He was the owner of a motor car, three carriages, two motor boats, and a number of cows and horses. The houses he owned were requisitioned by the Turkish Government for hospital purposes, and they used them for the worst cases, such as cholera, the Plague, and other dreadful diseases.

My Belgian friend was compelled to leave the house in which he was living, and seek refuge in a hotel in Constantinople. His own house was stripped, everything being taken away; his beautiful collection of rifles, pistols, pictures and furniture was stolen by the soldiers. His horses, cows, and in fact everything he had was taken away, and not even a requisition-bond handed to him. The Turks even appropriated his balance at the bank.

In stripping a man of his possessions, the Turk shows a thoroughness that would make a German green with envy. The Belgian has become a poor man who can hardly find food for his children. If it were not for some subjects of neutral countries, who had known him before the war, he and his family would be actually starving. The American Ambassador, Mr. Morgenthau, to whom was entrusted the care of these people, does not seem to be able to render them much assistance. Not only the Belgian of whom I have just spoken, but many others, complained to me that whenever they went to the American Embassy when something had been stolen from them by the Turks, they were put off with the assurance that nothing could possibly be done for them.

In all probability the French and British warship commanders were unaware of the Turkish method of dealing with the question of compensating the Faithful whose property had been damaged by bombardment. Whenever a house belonging to a Turk had been demolished by the French or British shells the property of one of the subjects of the enemy countries then living in Turkey was confiscated, and the owner with his family sent to the interior of Asia Minor. All his belongings were handed over to the Turk whose property had suffered through the bombardment.

The financial situation in Turkey is of an alarming nature, I found to my great delight. I myself had never been a real enemy of the Turks. I considered them a simple, good-hearted race, and in many ways superior to the inhabitants of the surrounding countries. What I found out during my last visit has, however, entirely changed my opinion. In many desirable ways they can claim the honour of equalling their German masters, but in cruelty, barbarism, and utter unscrupulousness they now excel even the Germans. No! I am no longer a friend of the Turks. Especially am I no friend of their Government.

When eight months previously I was in Turkey, I was astonished at the amount of gold that was in circulation. I had always heard that Turkey was such a poor country, and I was greatly surprised, when I entered a bank for the purpose of changing Austrian bank-notes, to find that I could get as much gold in exchange as I wanted, and I was puzzled, especially as that gold looked suspiciously new. I afterwards found that it was part of the gold that Germany had lent, or given, to her Turkish friend to get her to participate in the war. Gold had also been given for the purpose of paying requisitions, which were many, for the Turks as a result of the Balkan War had exhausted nearly all their war material. I found out that many of those requisitions had, however, not been paid. In fact, of the new war requisitions not one had been paid, most of the gold having been peculated by the Turkish officials in high places. The result was a bitter quarrel with the Germans, which, however, had been kept secret.

For obvious reasons the Germans refused to send any more gold—they had none themselves. Some months ago Enver Pasha went to Berlin to try and settle the affair, and his mission seems to have been successful.

On this visit to Constantinople I found the financial situation was critical. All the gold had disappeared, and, what is even more significant, silver was hardly to be obtained either. This is due to the fact that the new Treasury bonds recently issued by the Turkish Government are refused in the interior of Turkey, which is where the farms are situated. The Anatolian farmers promptly refused to accept paper money in exchange for their products, and the Turkish merchants, in order to purchase the harvest, etc., were compelled to pay the farmers in silver money. The result is that there is hardly any silver left in Constantinople, but there is any amount of it circulating in the interior of Asia Minor.

The shortage of currency has paralysed the Turkish trade, and therefore the Government had to think of something. Just a few days before I left Constantinople I witnessed the appearance of the funniest paper money I have ever seen. Just imagine the situation. In Turkey, on £1 notes (the original value of a £1 note is about 17s. or 18s.), even at the Government offices or State Railways, one has to lose about ten per cent. in exchange. To meet the shortage of currency the Turks decided it would be legal to cut a £1 note in half, so when I took my meal one day in the Tokatlian Restaurant, in the Pera Street, I received my change in this new fashion. It was a very odd sight to see a man get his knife out of his pocket and cut the bank-note in half.

It has always been my desire to see a Turkish woman face to face, unveiled, of course. They seem so mysterious with their covered faces, and one imagines them much nicer than they really are, on account of the mysterious way in which they go about. On my previous visit I had not succeeded in seeing one; this time I was more lucky. One day I entered the post-office in Stamboul, where no Europeans live, and went to the Poste Restante box to find if there were any letters for me. A young girl was answering my questions, and she was a pretty Oriental-looking creature. At first I took her for one of the innumerable Jewish or Grecian girls who are to be found in Constantinople. She spoke the French language very well, and after I had spoken for a few minutes I asked her if she were Grecian or Armenian. She answered me at once, "No, I am a Mussulman girl." "What!" I exclaimed, "are you Turkish, *real* Turkish?" "Yes, I am," she said, and then went on to tell me that during the last fortnight a few Mahommedan young girls had entered the Government service, and she told me that others were to follow. If all Turkish women are as charming as she was, then a harem must be far more interesting than I thought it could be.

Several times I had noticed black Turkish troops passing me in the streets, men of the typical African negro type, and I could not understand from what part of Turkey they had come. I soon found out, however, that they were not Turks at all, but French native soldiers who had been taken prisoners during the Gallipoli campaign. These soldiers, being Mahommedans, were soon turned into Turkish soldiers. The Turks treated them well, put them into Turkish uniforms, and now they fight against the French!

Tall and well-dressed German soldiers were on duty everywhere. A lot has been written about old men, belonging to the Landsturm, and boys, being taken prisoners on the Western front, but the Germans are not sending this class of men to the Near East. Their army in Constantinople consists of really first-class troops. It has been stated by the Salonika correspondent of *The Times* that there are 50,000 troops in Constantinople. That number may have passed through the city. In my opinion, arrived at after careful calculation, the number of German soldiers actually in Constantinople may be put down at about 10,000.

When I was in Constantinople eight months previously there was comparative gaiety in the city. It is extraordinary to see the difference that has been made by the absence of electricity and gas. It has at once closed theatres, cafés, kinemas, and all other places of amusement. Nearly all the shops are closed. With the cutting off of the coal supply the whole life of the city has thus been destroyed. In London there is at least some light, but in Constantinople the only means of getting about at night is by the aid of electric torches, the very smallest of which cost me 8s.

The condition of affairs in the city approached famine; the electric tramway service, as far as the public is concerned, has practically come to a standstill. I took careful note of the prices of necessaries; sugar is 5s. a pound, coffee 6s. a pound, and cigarettes have been advanced by 40 per cent. Anyone who knows Turkey will understand what this means for a people that smokes practically all day long. Matches are 3d. a box. The stock of paraffin oil has been exhausted, likewise that of chocolate, and all cheese, save the horrible Turkish variety, is no longer procurable. Mutton has advanced 40 per cent. in price and beef is not to be had. The small Turkish eggs, which used to cost one farthing each eight months ago, are now twopence each. Soap is ridiculously expensive, but the Turk does not suffer much in consequence! There is very little rice, but fish, of course, is as plentiful as ever, thanks to the unique situation of Constantinople.

Despite all these difficulties and inconveniences, the German War-Machine seems to move with its customary precision. If the Turkish citizen goes short of food the German private soldier gets his full ration every day. This is as it should be, according to the German view.

CHAPTER V

I INTERVIEW ENVER PASHA

> Germanising the Turkish War Office—Halil Bey—Wireless Disguised as a Circus—Enver Pasha Receives Me—The Turkish Napoleon—Something of a Dandy—"If the English Had Only Had the Courage"—"To Egypt!"—Turkey's Debt to Great Britain—Affairs Before Manners—A German Tribute to British Troops—Their Designs in the Suez Canal—German War Plans—Where to Kill Germans—The Baghdad Expedition—German Officers in Mufti.

The principal object of my visit to Constantinople was to find out from the Turks what were the German plans. I determined to take the bull by the horns, and accordingly called at the Turkish Foreign office to see Halil Bey, the Foreign Minister. It must be remembered that I was in possession of a personal introduction to him from the Turkish Ambassador in Vienna. After four unsuccessful attempts, I succeeded in seeing him by reason of my credentials, which have enabled me to gather so much valuable information. The Foreign Office, like every other Government department, is infested with Germans. Halil Bey, who received me courteously, is a prosperous-looking Turk, who might be described as fat. He was frankly pro-German.

"What we Turks need," he remarked, "is German business initiative. We do not possess it yet. Look what Germany did for Roumania; she has reorganised her and set her on her feet. Roumania is now rich and prosperous, and full of enterprise. The Germans are with us only for the duration of the war," he added, "and they will help Turkey to become a wealthy nation. See what they are doing for us in Anatolia. There we have 200 German non-commissioned officers teaching the people modern farming."

I decided that Halil Bey was an optimist, and a very poor student of history. Also an equally bad judge of German character.

My object in seeking out Halil Bey, however, was not so much to obtain his own opinions, as to get an introduction to Enver Pasha. I pressed the Foreign Minister very hard.

"It is my desire," I said, "to have a few words with the Napoleon of the Balkans."

"That," he replied, "is very difficult. Twenty or thirty Austrian and German journalists have been here, but the Minister of War has been so occupied that he has been unable to see any of them; but I will try," he added, and taking up the telephone he called up the War Minister, and had some laughing conversation with him in Turkish, the nature of which I did not understand. So far as I was concerned, it was obviously satisfactory, and I was told to go to the War Office on the following morning, when Enver Pasha would grant me an audience.

The Turkish War Office stands on the top of a hill in the very heart of Stamboul, the native quarter of the city. It is a huge squat building surrounded by a railing some five yards high. The hill commands a magnificent view of Stamboul and the Sea of Marmora; but to a poor and over-tired journalist, unable to procure a carriage, who has for half-an-hour toiled laboriously up the hill to reach his goal, the glories of nature are somewhat discounted.

During my previous visit to Constantinople I had made the acquaintance of the War Office, then sadly dirty and neglected and typically Turkish in appearance. Now everything was so changed as to be scarcely recognisable. Inside and out it had been redecorated. It was obviously the intention of the Germans that, however neglected the other Turkish Government buildings might be, the War Office was to be a place that would impress itself upon the imagination.

Again I was struck by the number of German officers to be seen, albeit in Turkish uniforms for the most part. They were to be seen everywhere, and clearly the entire direction of affairs was in their hands.

On my arrival I was ushered into an anteroom, where I spent a few minutes in conversation with Enver's German *aide-de-camp*.

As we sat chatting together I recalled an incident that occurred during my previous visit to the Turkish War Office in May, 1915. Through one of the windows I had noticed a huge mast belonging to the great wireless station of Osmanli.

"What do you think of it?" inquired a German lieutenant with whom I had been conversing. "With that wireless station we can communicate with Berlin."

I doubted this at the time, but I have since discovered that the statement was quite correct. I inquired if it were the wireless from the *Goeben*, deliberately assuming innocence in order to stimulate the German to further disclosure.

"Oh, no," was the reply, "ships do not carry masts of that size. This one came from Germany."

"From Germany!" I exclaimed. "But surely Roumania would not allow to pass a wireless apparatus. That would be a violation of neutrality."

The officer smiled, a German smile, a smile of superior knowledge. "Well," he replied, "as a matter of fact it was not passed as a wireless apparatus, but I will explain to you the little device that we used to get it there. We had to think out some plan, as we badly needed a strong apparatus, so we got it here as a circus!"

I laughed outright, but my companion did not appear to see anything funny in the incident. It seemed to strike him as clever rather than humorous—he was a typical German. Humour does not exist where the needs of the Fatherland are concerned.

Presently an electric bell rang, summoning the *aide-de-camp*, who conducted me into the War Minister's presence. My first impression of Enver Pasha was that he was on very good terms with himself. He is a small man, standing perhaps some five feet five inches, with coal-black eyes, black moustache, and generally rather handsome features. He is about thirty-five years of age, but looks younger, and has obviously taken great care of himself. On his face was a pleased, contented expression that never for one moment left it. I could not say whether this was habitual or whether it was assumed for my special benefit. He was well-dressed and well-groomed, with something of the dandy about him; low down on the left breast he wore the Iron Cross of the First Class. He spoke German perfectly, Halil speaks only French.

Enver smiled as he shook hands with me, not only at my fez, but at my card which was printed in Turkish characters. There was a merry twinkle in his eye, and he had an extremely easy manner. It is said that he models himself, not upon the Great War Lord but upon Napoleon, even to the extent of riding a white charger. The general impression in Constantinople was that he has no little conceit of himself. Never for one moment did he allow me to forget that he was graciously giving me some of his valuable time. His first act was to produce a big gold cigarette case, from which he invited me to take a cigarette, having first carefully selected one himself. He then leaned back comfortably in his arm-chair and awaited my questions.

To make him talk I asked whether it was true that Great Britain was prepared to make a separate peace with Turkey, and, if so, what would be the result of such overtures.

"It is too late," he replied, smiling. "They may have had that design, and it might have succeeded; but we learn that the Entente"—or as he called them jocularly the mal-Entente—"Powers have designs to hand over Constantinople to Russia, and that compelled us to remain with the Central Powers."

Referring to the Gallipoli campaign, he said: "If the English had only had the courage to rush more ships through the Dardanelles they would have got to

Constantinople, but their delay enabled us thoroughly to fortify the Peninsula, and in six weeks' time we had taken down there over two hundred Austrian Skoda guns.

"But," he continued, "even had the British ships got to Constantinople it would not have availed them very much. Our plan was to retire our army to the surrounding hills and to Asia Minor and leave the city at their mercy. They would not have destroyed it, and the result would have been simply an *impasse*. With the Germans we can strike at the British Empire through the Suez Canal. Our motto is, 'To Egypt!'"

I told him that in my country we found it extremely difficult to realise that Turkey was actually at war with England and France, seeing that but for the efforts of these two countries Turkey would long since have ceased to exist as a separate kingdom in Europe.

"That is quite correct (sie haben recht)," he replied without pausing to think. But in the same breath he murmured, "Whatever England did for Turkey was not dictated out of love, but rather from consideration for her own interests. England feared the competition of Russia in the Mediterranean."

I was a little suspicious of Enver's complacent attitude, but I believe he was sincere in what he said to me. I watched him very carefully when he told me that the sacrifice of a few more ships would have got the English to Constantinople, and I am convinced that this is his firm opinion. I could not help thinking of the pity of it all, and that 200,000 casualties might have been saved by a little more enterprise. I learned that this opinion was general in Constantinople, even in high diplomatic quarters.

At the end of ten minutes Enver rose and remarked: "You must excuse me now, I am busy." He shook hands with me and abruptly left the room. I was a little surprised at this, but concluded that in his many responsibilities he had never had the leisure in which to study manners, and the courtesy due even to a journalist. Had I been English I could better have understood his attitude; for, some years ago, he visited England, where he did not receive the attention he expected. The result was that he returned to Constantinople strongly anti-British.

Enver's view as to the possibility of Great Britain forcing the Dardanelles, had they shown a little more vigour and indifference to the loss of a few ships, I found echoed by the German officers whom I met both at the Pera Palace and the Continental Hotel, where I stayed on my return from Asia Minor, only in their case it was more vehemently expressed. The Turks have no real dislike for the English and none for the French, although all French words have been removed from the shop-signs in Constantinople.

German officers, however, were very free in expressing their loathing of the British, though full of admiration for the fighting capacity of their soldiers. On every hand I heard the remark that they wished they had British, Australian and Canadian Tommies to command. The general view expressed in Constantinople is to the effect that the united German-Turkish army will destroy the Suez Canal from one end to the other, if necessary, filling it up with its ancient sand and thus render it impassable.

"But if you do that," I remarked to more than one of them, "the British will merely return to their old route to India *via* the Cape of Good Hope."

Never once did they vouchsafe an answer to this. The German has an extraordinary capacity for seeing no further than his particular goal. He is a creature of cries "To Paris!" "To Calais!" "To Warsaw!" "To Egypt!"; and when he finds himself baulked he forgets his object, just as a child forgets a toy when something more interesting presents itself.

One and all, however, admitted that there was no chance of the Germans getting to Paris. Their contention was—and it must be remembered that many of them had been fighting in the West—that they had effectually walled off the English and French armies and rendered them to all intents and purposes impotent, thus enabling themselves together with their allies—Austrian, Turkish, Bulgarian, and Arabian—to operate freely on the Eastern front.

As I have said, my instructions were to find out what were the German plans in the East. With this object I mingled freely with as many Germans and Turks as possible. I lost no opportunity of entering into conversation with anyone who showed the least inclination to converse. Fortunately I speak French perfectly, and German almost as well. French enabled me to talk to the Turks, and my German permitted me to "get close," as the Americans say, not only to the German soldiers, but to officers and civilians, who are stationed at, or are passing through, Constantinople on their way to Asia Minor.

It appears to be part of the German economic plan to turn Turkey into a great German dependency, and to force the Turk to cultivate the soil, which in some places is the richest in the world. The true humour of the situation will develop when the Turk discovers what he has let himself in for. As to the German military plans, they are, so far as I could gather, three in number. My own view is that they will attempt the whole three simultaneously, and then allow them to develop as fortune may decide. These plans are (1) the Baghdad-Persia-India plan; (2) the Caucasus plan, with which to tackle the Russians; (3) Egypt and the Suez Canal plan.

One afternoon a German said to me, "If the English and French only knew, the proper place to kill Germans is between Nieuport in Belgium and Mülhausen in Alsace; but owing to their inferior staff work, lack of munitions, fear of our guns, gas, mines, and machine-guns, they leave us comparatively quiet in the Western theatre, and enable us to menace the line of communication to India and the ridiculous Townshend Expedition, which will never get to Baghdad."

There is among the German officers a general contempt for the English and French, particularly the English, staff work. At the Sachim Pasha Hotel in Stamboul I encountered a pleasant old Turk who spoke French extremely well. He was the Vali of Baghdad (a sort of Justice of the Peace, I believe), who had come to report to the Germans the condition of the English and Turkish forces. What he said was practically a repetition of what Enver had said to me a few days previously about Gallipoli: "We were very alarmed when we heard they were coming," he remarked, "for our defences were in a bad condition, and we had nothing but a few old guns. Our spies, however told us that General Townshend's force was a small one, and we therefore took courage and held the English in check until we could get our reinforcements; now, thanks to Allah, they will never reach our holy city, their relief force is too late."

It is not for me to offer advice to the British Government. As I have said, I love the country just as I hate the Germans, but I wish the British Ministers could appreciate how often the term "too late," in connection with the operations of the Allies, has cropped up during this journey of mine.

The German authorities in Constantinople were urged by the people at Baghdad to send every available man there, whereas the immediate wish of the Turks is to get to the Suez Canal and so regain their fair province of Egypt and the Nile. Turkish sentiment combined with German hatred of England may probably precipitate the immediate advance on the Canal. I have been told frequently since my return to England that this is impossible, that it is only "bluff." I remember the same things being said when Enver Pasha announced, months ago, that the Germans were coming to relieve Constantinople. My own opinion—which, of course, may be worth nothing, but it is formed as the result of talking to scores of Turks and Germans in Constantinople and Asia Minor—is that unless there be great combined efforts in France by the British and French, and in the Caucasus by the Russians, the Germans and Turks may achieve one—at least one—of their three objects, possibly two, perhaps all three even. The determining factors are the pressure by the hated British Navy and greater activity in France, Belgium, and Russia.

At four o'clock every afternoon the German officers, who are constantly arriving from Berlin at the Pera Palace Hotel to receive their instructions, remove their military clothes and appear in mufti. Here again we have evidence of German subtlety. No man in the world loves his uniform as does the German officer, but, as one waggish Bavarian lieutenant said to me, "We must not give the Turks the impression that we are a flight of German locusts. We do not want the Galata Bridge to look like Unter den Linden all the time, so as soon as we have finished our duty we go about as civilians." They are wise. Constantinople already looks quite German enough; that is, to Turkish eyes. There are German newspapers printed in the city, there are the crews of the *Goeben* and *Breslau* wearing the Turkish fez, and of the submarines, and swarms of miscellaneous Germans, all with their particular object in view. These facts in themselves are enough to cause misgiving in the heart of the most pronouncedly pro-German Turk. My own impression is that whatever may be the result of the war the Germans are getting such a hold on the Near East that it will be next to impossible to drive them out. Money is scarce in Germany, but the Germans seem to have plenty to spend in Turkey and Asia Minor.

CHAPTER VI

I VISIT ASIA MINOR

A Remarkable Railway Station—I Leave for Konia—The Anatolian Railway—How to Get to Baghdad—Elaborate Instructions—Necessity for Caution—English and French Prisoners—Instructing the Turk in the Arts of Peace—A Noisy Sleeper—Hamburg's Hatred of Great Britain—Sops to Austria and Turkey—Field-Marshal Von der Goltz—I Return to Constantinople.

After I had been nine days in Constantinople I determined to undertake what I clearly saw would be the most dangerous portion of my journey. At that time I did not anticipate encountering the Kaiser and his detective bodyguard at Nish.

I knew that for ordinary civil travellers the Anatolian Railway is closed, because the whole of Asia Minor is what we call here in "the War Zone." After my interview with Enver Pasha, however, I thought it would not be so difficult to get permission to travel into the interior of Turkey, and in fact, after two days' ceaseless effort and many hours spent in ante-rooms, I was lucky enough to secure the so much-desired permission. It was stated on my passport in Turkish characters, under the stamp of the Turkish War Office, that I was to be allowed to travel in the military zone—in other words, that I could go into Asia Minor.

I took the ferry boat across the Bosphorus to the Haidar Pasha railway station, a palatial edifice, the starting place for all the great German ventures in the East. It has been built quite recently by a German company, and stands there as a monument of the enterprise and ability of that astonishing nation. Haidar Pasha itself is a mere village on the Sea of Marmora, and the station stands out in one of the most beautiful positions of its kind in the world. The heart of every patriotic Teuton thrills as he struts about the great hall, and reads the various notices in his native tongue.

The rest of the world has a good deal to learn from the German railway station, and this one at Haidar Pasha is an object-lesson in cleanliness to the Turks. The surrounding country looks poor, all the houses are small and ill-kept, and the more one looks at the beautiful station the more obvious is its contrast with its surroundings. It must be remembered that every Turkish or German soldier going to the Caucasus, Mesopotamian, or Egyptian front will have to pass through the station of Haidar Pasha, the terminus of the Anatolian, and in fact all the Turkish railways in Asia.

My dark complexion, coupled with my habitual wearing of the fez, caused me to attract less attention than would otherwise have been the case. I had fortunately struck up a slight acquaintance with Enver Pasha's German *aide-de-camp*, and he most kindly obliged me with official directions of how to get to Baghdad, where to stop, what to pay at the so-called hotels, and so forth. I can only hope, for his own peace of mind, that he never reads this book.

This list of instructions is a typical example of German thoroughness, and is printed in French because, although Germans now swarm in Turkey and Asia Minor, the only language possible for a visiting traveller in out of the way places is French—that is, provided he does not know Turkish.

I regard the document as of such interest that I reproduce it below, together with a translation.

BULLETIN DES RENSEIGNEMENTS

sur le voyage de Haidar-Pacha à Rees-el-Ain.

1. Départ de Haidar-Pacha, arrivée le soir à Eski-Chehir; Hôtel Tadia (Mme. Tadia).

2. Départ d'Eski-Chehir, arrivée à Konia; Hôtel de la Gare construit par la Société (Mme. Soulié).

3. Départ de Konia, arrivée à Bozanti. Il n'y a à Bozanti qu'un simple han.

4. Trajet en voiture de Bozanti à Tarsus, 70 kilom. en 10 à 12 heures sur bonne chaussée. Les voitures doivent être commandées d'avance au Handji de Bozanti ou à Tarsus, si l'on veut poursuivre le voyage sans arrêt à Bozanti. Prix des voitures, de Ltqs 2 à 5 suivant les circonstances. Entre Bozanti et Tarsus il y a plusieurs Khans où l'on peut à la rigueur passer la nuit: Sary Cheih, Mezarolouk, Yéni-Han. Il se recommande d'emmener son lit de camp et de se pourvoir d'approvisionnements et de boissons suffisants.

5. Tarsus, environ ¾ d'heure avant d'y arriver on traverse la ligne du M.T.A. à la Halte de Kulek-Bognaz; à Tarsus 3 hôtels: Sérai Hotelli, Osmanli, et Stamboul (10 p. par lit), en outre restaurant "Bélédie."

6. Départ de Tarsus, arrivée à Mamouré. Mamouré n'est qu'une station d'étape militaire. Aucun hôtel ni han. Les voyageurs qui n'ont pas de tente à leur disposition peuvent passer la nuit chez de simples cafedjis, où ils trouvent quelques vivres, mais où ils ne peuvent obtenir de lits. Il est

donc préférable pour les voyageurs non munis de tente et de lit de camp de s'arrêter à Osmanié pour y passer la nuit. Hôtels: Ismyr et Ahmed (5 p. par lit). Les tenanciers de ces hôtels procurent les voitures nécessaires pour le voyage à Radjou. Prix des voitures 2 à 5 Ltqs. suivant les circonstances.

7. Trajet en voiture d'Osmanié à Radjou. Environ 110 kil. en 2 jours sur route carrossable, qui est une pendant la bonne saison: 1er jour; par Hassan bey et le col de l'Amanus à Entilli (environ 50 kil.); à Entilli point d'hôtels, rien que de simples cafedjis. Les voyageurs peuvent aussi passer la première nuit à Islahié à environ 12 kilom. d'Entilli; à Entilli, siège d'un caza, bureau d'étape militaire, plusieurs Hans avec des lits (10 p. per lit.) 2ème jour: de Entilli resp. Islahié à Radjou (60 resp. 48 kil.); à Radjoué ni hôtel ni hans; rien que des cafedjis.

8. De Radjou à Halep: le même jour (différents hôtels).

9. De Halep à Rees-el-Ain (le même jour). Siège d'un caza. Quelques Hans sans lits; rien que des cafedjis.

10. De Rees-el-Ain à Bagdad. Trajet qui s'offectue en 10 à 12 jours.

Recommandations spéciales: Lit de camp ou matelas indispensable. Il se recommande d'emmener aussi une tente. Malles doivent être de construction très solide et ne doivent pas excéder le poids de 60 kilogrs. par pièce. Au lieu de malles on peut prendre des valises ou des sacs de voyage. Le transport usuel se fait par voiture "Yaili," qui est toujours préférable au voyage par cheval. Se munir de vêtements chauds pour la nuit et d'approvisionnements et de boissons suffisants. Ne pas oublier une petite pharmacie de campagne. L'eau qu'on trouve en cours de route est souvent nuisible à la santé.

[*Translation.*]

DIRECTIONS

For the journey from Haidar Pasha to Ras-el-Ain.

1. Leave Haidar Pasha, arrive in evening at Eskishehr; Hotel Tadia, Mme. Tadia.

2. Leave Eskishehr, arrive Konia; Station Hotel built by the company, Mme. Sulieh.

3. Leave Konia, arrive Bozanti; only a simple inn.

4. By carriage or car, Bozanti to Tarsus, 44 miles in ten or twelve hours on good road. Vehicles should be ordered beforehand from Handji of Bozanti or at Tarsus if you wish to avoid delay at Bozanti. Fare £T2 to £T5 (£T1 nominally 17s. 6d. to 18s.), according to circumstances. Between Bozanti and Tarsus several inns to sleep at in emergency; Sary Cheih, Mezarolukl, Yeni-Han. Better take a camp bed and enough food and drink.

5. Tarsus, about three-quarters of an hour before arrival, cross the Tarsus-Aleppo line at the Halt Kulek-Boghaz. Three hotels at Tarsus: Serai, Osmanli, and Stambul, 10 piastres (1s. 8d.) a bed. Also a restaurant Beledieh.

6. Leave Tarsus, arrive Mamureh. This only a military post. No hotel or inn. Travellers without a tent may pass the night in the cafés, where they can get food, but no beds. Better if you have no tent or bed to stop at Osmanieh. Hotels Ismyr, Ahmed, 5 piastres (10d.) a bed. The hotel proprietors can get vehicles for the journey to Radju. Fares, £T2 to £T5, according to circumstances.

7. Journey by car or carriage, Osmanieh to Radju, about 70 miles in two days on a drivable road, which is good in the good season.

1st day: Hassan Bey and Pass of Amanus to Entilli, about 32 miles. At Entilli no hotels, only simple cafés. You can pass the first night at Islahieh, about 7½ miles from Entilli. Entilli district headquarters, military post, several inns with beds; 10 piastres a bed.

2nd day: Entilli (or Islahieh) to Radju, 38 (or 31½) miles. Radju, no hotels or inns, only cafés.

8. Radju to Aleppo same day. Various hotels.

9. Aleppo to Ras-el-Ain same day. District headquarters. Several inns without beds, only cafés.

10. Ras-el-Ain to Baghdad. Journey can be done in 10 to 12 days.

> Special advice: Camp bed or mattress indispensable. Advisable to take a tent. Trunks ought to be strongly made and weigh not over 120 lbs. each. Instead of trunks you may take bags or suit cases. The usual way is by the vehicle Yaili, always preferable to horseback. Get warm clothes for night and enough food and drink. Don't forget a little medicine chest. It is often risky to drink the water found on the way.

There is naturally far less danger of Secret Service officers in a crowded city than in small towns. In Constantinople I was but one of thousands of strangers passing to and fro, and that at a time of great change in the history of the Turkish capital. The arrival, however, of a stranger in a village sets every local busybody talking and speculating as to where he has come from and why he has come. And this brings him into conflict with, or at least under the suspicion of, some blundering minor official. Quite possibly this person, zealous in his desire to show his authority and his patriotism, may, by virtue of his blundering, stumble across something that his superiors have quite overlooked. Such a thing had happened to me already on a previous occasion.

I therefore determined to be more than ever careful, and to leave nothing whatever to chance. I was desirous of getting as far as possible along the Baghdad Railway, not only to examine the line itself, but to talk to the passengers *en route*. People of strange countries become companionable, and I have often found that there is more to be learned in a railway carriage during a comparatively short journey, than from a long stay in a city. There is a bond of sympathy between travellers, just as there is between smokers, that causes them after a few hours, sometimes even after only a few minutes, to become communicative. I wanted to get to Aleppo, but I came to the conclusion that I should probably never return if I penetrated too far on the road to Baghdad.

The train for Eski-Shehr, which is the junction for the Caucasian Railway, *via* Angora, left at four in the afternoon. Turkish soldiers on their way to the Caucasian front to fight the Russians go by rail only as far as Angora, the rest of the journey being made on foot. The roads are terribly bad, but the Turkish soldier philosophically overcomes all the difficulties he encounters, for he is justly famous for his stout heart and his capacity to endure hardships of every description.

In Angora, I believe, the English prisoners are confined. I have no evidence of this beyond a chance remark I heard whilst waiting for the train at Eski-Shehr. I know for a fact that French prisoners are in Angora. Later, at Konia, I saw some 300 French prisoners, deplorably neglected, I regret to say, with little food, and dying like flies. The insanitary condition of that camp was beyond description. The Turks are perhaps not naturally cruel, or, at least, they confine their atrocities to Armenia. They have their own particular views as regards prisoners in general. Turkish prisoners in Turkish prisons are not well treated. After all, a prisoner is not a very important factor in the Turkish mind, and it should be remembered that the food shortage extends throughout the whole area of German operations, always excepting the German soldier himself. Even at the beautiful station of Haidar Pasha I could not get a mouthful of bread or even a biscuit. The only refreshment obtainable was unlimited German beer, produced by a local German brewery.

The journey to Eski-Shehr was pleasant, although the trains were slow and stopped for a considerable time at each station. There are no express trains on the Baghdad Railway. There was, however, no paint on the windows of the carriages, for which I was devoutly thankful, and the carriages themselves were quite comfortable. As we sped along I was much struck by the number of German non-commissioned officers that I saw working and cultivating the land, which between Constantinople and Konia is for the most part fertile, in co-operation with the Turkish farmers. It was explained to me that more than 200 of these non-commissioned officers had been sent to Turkey with the sole purpose of teaching the Turkish farmers how to cultivate their ground. This, again, is typical of German methods, but it has another significance. If Berlin did not believe in the good faith of the Turks, and were not convinced that Germany will remain the unofficial masters of Turkey, all this trouble would certainly not be taken to instruct the people of Asia Minor in the art of agriculture. There is nothing philanthropic about the Germans.

All along the route until Konia was reached I saw these German non-commissioned officers, and whenever the train stopped some of them rushed up to the carriages asking for German newspapers, believing that all the passengers came from the Fatherland, as, indeed, some of them had.

My fellow-passengers were typical of the German invasion of the East. There were among them two merchants from Hamburg, going to bring back Persian products. They talked particularly about copper. At the hotel in Konia I had to sleep in the same room with one of them, and I was desperately afraid lest I might talk in my sleep, and, indeed, when a Turk came to awaken me in the morning I inadvertently called out, "Come in." The good Hamburger was lying flat on his back, sleeping noisily, and I thanked the good luck that seemed to protect me for sending me as a companion one who was so hearty a sleeper. That Hamburger impressed upon me in no uncertain manner the meaning of sea power. The British are not actually popular in Berlin, as is well known; but the feelings of Berliners are mild and gentle in comparison with those of the inhabitants of the desolated port of Hamburg.

I have seen it stated in the English newspapers that supplies are getting into Germany in spite of the British Fleet, and there are many evidences of this fact in Germany. On the other hand, however, these supplies have to meet the consumptive power of some seventy millions of people. A little, too, is doled out now and then to the Austrians, as if to keep them quiet, but it is very little, and I suppose that even the Turkish officials get a small percentage for the same purpose. The balance goes to the German Army, for that must never be short of anything. It is obvious that if you must be a German, the wisest thing is to be a German soldier.

I have seen it stated that von Mackensen will take charge of the Turkish-German forces at Aleppo, the place from which the expedition to the Suez Canal will start. At present Djamil Pasha, formerly Turkish Minister of Marine, is in command. Travellers who had come from Aleppo told me that the combined German and Turkish forces there numbered 80,000, but I am not in a position to guarantee the accuracy of these figures. What I do know is that there is everywhere an air of general activity and preparation. Long trains full of new railway and telegraph material, rails, small bridges, and numbers of locomotives are to be encountered everywhere. The plodding, persistent Prussian is prodding his Turkish slaves into such action as has never before been known to them. It is incredible that those in high places among the Turks can conceive it possible that they will ever be able to shake off the German yoke. There is to be seen *en route* a great amount of light railway rolling stock, and I was assured that it was intended for the construction of the railway that will cross the desert to bring the Turkish-German armies face to face with the British on the Canal.

Field-Marshal von der Goltz is at Baghdad. He is one of the oldest German generals with one of the youngest German staffs. At Constantinople they say that the old man is merely a figure head, but he is extremely popular with the young men about him.

At Konia, for reasons that I cannot explain, I thought it advisable to run no further risk, and so I returned to Constantinople. It was very fortunate for me that I did so, otherwise I might have missed the Banquet at Nish, and I should not have earned the name of "The Man who Dined With the Kaiser."

CHAPTER VII

CONSTANTINOPLE FROM WITHIN

A City of Maimed and Wounded—I See the Sultan—Enver's Popularity—Talaat Bey the Real Administrator—Gallipoli Day—Constantinople "Mafficks"—The Return of the Ten Thousand—How the *Goeben* and *Breslau* Escaped—Their Fateful Arrival at Constantinople—German Privileges—Mendacities of the Turkish Press—The Egyptian Situation—A German Camel Corps—The Turks a Formidable Factor.

To me Constantinople seemed to be a city of maimed and wounded. One morning I strolled out of my hotel, intending to take a carriage to Stamboul, one of those strange vehicles drawn by two lean but vigorous horses that still remain on the streets for hire. From twenty-five to thirty carriages passed me as I stood vainly endeavouring to persuade one of the drivers to pull up. They took not the slightest notice of my gesticulations, but continued precipitately on their way. I was curious to know the reason for this, and on my return to the hotel I inquired of the porter. He informed me that the carriages were going to the Bosphorus to take up the wounded arriving from different battlefields. "After what you have told me," I remarked, "I shall be afraid of using a carriage in Constantinople." But shaking his head, the porter replied dispassionately, "Do not be afraid. By order of the Germans, every one of these carriages must be disinfected after use." "The East is the East and the West is the West," I meditated as I passed into the hotel. It would be interesting to have the frank opinion of the highly-placed Turk upon the "thoroughness" of their German allies.

I very soon discovered that every big building in the city had been turned into a hospital, one of the biggest being the Lyceum. All the beautiful houses belonging to the wealthy English and French residents, which overlook the Bosphorus, have been commandeered for the Red Crescent, the occupants being obliged under Turkish war regulations to live in hotels.

The Sultan is a mere figure-head, as is well known. One Friday I saw him walking from his palace to a mosque a little distance away—he has given up taking the longer journey to the Aya Sofia for fear of assassination—and his fat, heavy appearance suggested to me that the Turks knew their business when they removed all power from his hands. In the old days a Sultan could not make his appearance in the streets without its being the occasion for a great demonstration. That was yesterday; now popular enthusiasm was for Enver Pasha when he accompanied the Commander of the Faithful. The potentate himself might be persuaded that the acclamations were for his holy person, but everyone else knew better. I was told that the Sultan leaves everything to Talaat Bey and to Enver Pasha. To me the Sultan looked like an unidealised copy of one of Rembrandt's Rabbis.

Enver may claim to be the power behind the throne, but the real ruler of Turkey is that shrewd statesman Talaat Bey, who, although a great Germanophile, is credited with the belief in the ultimate victory of the Entente Powers. This conviction on the part of Talaat may account for some of the rumours circulated in the Balkans to the effect that he would be not unwilling to conclude a separate peace.

I was in Constantinople when the evacuation of Gallipoli was announced. The town was gay with flags, mobs passed up and down the streets shouting. Notices in Turkish and German were exhibited everywhere. Special newspaper bulletins were being rushed hither and thither by ragged boys. The Turks, who are never over-prodigal of truth, announced the evacuation as a great victory for their soldiers, which had resulted in the English being driven into the sea. Although I had no other news than that supplied by the official proclamation, I was not in the least disturbed, knowing full well the Turkish character. Had there been a great victory there would have been prisoners, and the German knows too well the advantages of clever stage management not to produce these for the edification of the cheering crowd.

Three days later, when Constantinople had to some extent recovered from its mafficking, there passed through the streets about 10,000 of the weariest soldiers it has ever been my lot to see, a long bedraggled line, most of them stumbling along as if scarcely able to stand for fatigue. The people did not know where they had come from. Had they been aware that these poor wretches were some of the stout defenders of Gallipoli they might have given them a warmer cheer. As it was, I saw little or no enthusiasm, although here and there people ran out to give the men cigarettes.

The sight of these utterly worn-out soldiers lingered with me all day. Some of them were so exhausted that they could proceed no further, and had to be lifted up and half carried, half dragged along by their more stalwart comrades. They carried neither rifles nor knapsacks, these following behind in carts. It was interesting to note to what an extent the German officering of the Turkish forces has been carried. For every Turkish officer that passed by in that brown and miserable procession that smacked so little of victory, there were two German officers. The Turks may be entitled to all the satisfaction that the British evacuation of Gallipoli has given them, but I am sure that if the Anzac heroes, for instance, had been present with me the morning I stood watching the long war-worn line, they would have been comforted by the knowledge that however great the hardships and privations they themselves had suffered, those of the foe had been as bad, if not worse. It was obvious that some time would elapse before these men were sufficiently rested to be fit for active service once more, and this in spite of the fact that the Turkish soldier is famous for his remarkable recuperative powers.

I have seen it stated in the newspapers (February 13th, 1916), that large reinforcements of Turkish troops are being sent to Mesopotamia. This seems to confirm my view that several weeks' rest would be necessary before the men who fought so well at Gallipoli would be ready for active service again. Even these must be picked men, for it is a long and tedious march from Aleppo to Baghdad over roads that the word "wretched" utterly fails to describe.

At Stenia, in the Bosphorus, I saw both of those mystery ships, the *Goeben* and the *Breslau*, lying at anchor; probably there were never two ships in all the world about which so much that is inaccurate has been written. The *Goeben* was in a bad state, and kept afloat only by means of the crudest contrivances, shell-holes being filled in with cement. It is obvious that the authorities, be they Turkish or German, do not regard her as likely to be of much further assistance to them, for several of her big guns have been removed for use on land. The *Breslau*, on the other hand, is in good condition, and as I saw her riding at anchor she looked very spick and span, having recently received a new coat of grey paint. She is a finely-built ship, and looks capable of rendering a very good account of herself.

The stories of how the *Goeben* and *Breslau* evaded the Allied fleets are legion. A Turkish deputy gave me one account which I relate for what it is worth. According to him it would appear that the two ships had taken refuge in Messina, and that outside the three-mile limit there waited 24 Allied ships of war, like hounds ready to pounce upon their prey. The prospect of escape seemed hopeless, so hopeless in fact that the commander of the *Breslau* proposed exceeding his time allowance in a neutral port so that his ship might be interned. The commander of the *Goeben*, however, was determined to make an effort to get away, and being the senior officer his less courageous comrade had no choice but to acquiesce. They waited until night, and then steamed away, keeping as near to the coast as possible, and were never overhauled. It was their arrival in the Dardanelles, the Turkish deputy assured me, that finally induced Turkey to join the Central Powers, the Turks believing that with the addition of these two fine ships to their navy they would be more than a match for the Russian Fleet in the Black Sea.

One day I made a curious discovery, not without its significance. In crossing the Galata Bridge a toll of one penny is demanded, which all the Faithful must pay, and likewise the Infidels. An exception, however, was made in the case of the Germans, who are exempt, and for this very interesting reason. When the bridge was damaged by the torpedo of a British submarine some time ago, the Turks were in a quandary to know how to repair it, having no engineers of their own capable of undertaking such work. In their difficulties they turned, as usual, to their German friends, who readily agreed to undertake the work, and the damage was accordingly made good. When the bill was presented from Berlin, however, the Turks wrung their hands, and with tears in their eyes expostulated that, although they had the best intentions in the world, they had no money.

The result was that the Germans had to allow the bill to remain owing, but by way of getting some acknowledgment for their trouble and the expense that they had incurred, they made it a condition that all German subjects should be allowed to cross the bridge free of charge. This I was able to prove by a very simple test, for on presenting myself to the tollkeepers and speaking German, I was immediately allowed to pass without any demand of the customary penny. It amused me to think that the real inhabitants of Constantinople should have to pay for the privilege that was accorded free to those who had usurped their authority.

The attitude of the Turks in regard to truth is too well known to require comment, but the lying qualities with which their press seems to be inspired are worthy of the word inspiration. To believe anything seen in a Turkish newspaper postulates a simplicity and credulity which, charming enough in themselves, are scarcely calculated to help its possessor in the struggle for existence. For instance, in Has Keiul, on the Golden Horn, a big powder factory was destroyed by a tremendous explosion; the Turkish newspapers charmingly described how three persons had been killed and six wounded, and that only two houses in addition to the factory had been destroyed. I determined to test this statement, and I found on visiting what is the Jewish quarter, that the whole neighbourhood was in ruins. Two thousand people at least had been killed, and, although my visit was not made until a fortnight after the explosion, search-parties were still digging dead bodies out of the ruins. The Turk himself is not entirely devoid of thoroughness.

Just as I was preparing to leave Constantinople rumours of the big Russian offensive in the Caucasus were coming through. Almost the last thing I saw were five battalions of Turks, splendidly equipped and with 1916 rifles, leaving for the Caucasus front.

I wish I were able to persuade the British public of the seriousness of the Egyptian situation. What most surprised me on my return to this country was the incredulity of the general public with regard to the German threat against Egypt and India. I am a neutral with no axe to grind, but I have a great respect and affection for a country where I have received nothing but kindness, and I view with alarm this dangerous and apathetic frame of mind. All that I saw in Constantinople, as in Asia Minor, convinces me that the Turks are serious in their intended invasions, and as the whole affair will be under German management it will, after the manner of the Germans, be done thoroughly. I feel that I shall have achieved something if any words of mine can dispel the illusion on the subject which seems to prevail everywhere.

Nothing is to be left to chance, and the Germans have taken the precaution, as a preparation for the Egyptian Expedition, of training 4,000 German soldiers to ride camels, the instruction being given at Hagenbeck's Menagerie at Hamburg. All those who know Egypt will appreciate the value of a body of 4,000 camelry. Aleppo is to be the starting point, and a glance at the map of Syria will show its importance. I shall be greatly surprised if within the next few months something is not heard of Djemal Pasha, who is in command there. When I was in Constantinople the name of the redoubtable von Mackensen was freely mentioned in connection with the leadership of this expedition, but other work will most likely be found for him.

The Turks are still a very formidable factor in the situation, and have to be seriously reckoned with. Their losses may be, and undoubtedly have been, very great, but there are plenty of men still available. As a matter of fact, all able-bodied men are being called to the colours. That alone should give Great Britain an indication of the magnitude of the task that lies before the Allies. Turkey may be one of the weaker members against the combination of the Entente Powers, but she is nevertheless very strong, and hourly growing stronger under the masterful domination of the German military mind.

The language difficulty in Turkey is rather amusing. Germany has done its best to implant its own tongue upon its unfortunate allies, but with very poor success. It was a constant source of amusement to me to hear German officers ordering their dinners in French. Everywhere in Constantinople French is spoken; even the tramway tickets are printed in French and Turkish. Waiters, shopkeepers, officers, sometimes even the man in the street speaks French as well as his own language. Frequently I would go to the rescue of German soldiers and sailors in shops who could not make themselves understood.

The German opinion of the Turks is very well shown by the following little episode. I was in conversation one day with two A.B.'s of the famous cruiser *Emden*. As a souvenir one of them gave me the ribbon from his cap with the *Emden* scroll upon it. He informed me that it was his original intention to give it to his mother, but he was now convinced that he would never return to the Fatherland alive, consequently I received it as a compliment in return for the beer and cigars I had given him. This sailor was communicative to the extent of saying, "We have lost nearly all our Colonies, and I am sure that we shall lose the last one, but we are going to make Turkey our newest and best colony." I heard similar remarks from other Germans.

CHAPTER VIII

THE "UNTERSEE" GERMAN

My Kiel Acquaintance—Submarines by Rail—German Submarines at Constantinople—My Voyage of Discovery—The Exploit of U51—Captain von Hersing—German Hero-worship—A Daring Feat—A Modest German!—Von Hersing in England—The German Naval Officer—His Opinion of the British Navy—A Regrettable Incident—Dr. Ledera Imprisoned—I Encounter an Austrian Spy—He Confides to me his Methods—The Carelessness of British Consuls.

An axiom, and a very valuable one, for a man employed in secret service work for a newspaper should be to stay always at the best hotel in any city at which he is making investigations. For one thing, big fish swim in large lakes; for another, the visitors at large hotels are less noticed and less likely to be suspected than those at smaller places.

At the Pera Palace Hotel I had many interesting conversations with German officers, for whom I had to swallow my dislike for reasons of policy. They complained to me bitterly of the absence of amusement, for all the theatres and picture palaces were closed, and there was no distraction whatever for the apostles of "Frightfulness." I was always ready with sympathy, and we got on very well together.

The officer of the Polish Legion at Vienna who told me about the terrible fate of the 28th Regiment, had introduced me to a German foreman-constructor of submarines, who had come from the famous Germania Shipyard at Kiel. He was a typical German of the boasting type, and as the result of a little judicious handling, some beer, and a great deal of flattery, of which any traveller in Germany has to take with him an unlimited supply, I soon discovered a great deal as to the mystery of the German submarines in the Sea of Marmora. Of the small type there are, I believe, not more than four; very likely the number has been increased since I left Turkey, as I will explain.

A little more than a year ago the English newspapers were engaged in discussing the possibility of Germans carrying submarines by rail. Whilst this was in progress the Germans had already solved the problem, and had conclusively proved that submarines of the smaller type can easily be manufactured in one place in sections and carried hundreds of miles by rail to another, where, with the aid of experts, they can be fitted together. As my new acquaintance informed me, Germany had already done this most successfully.

I proved the accuracy of the man's statement when I was at Constantinople, as I saw no less than four German U boats, Nos. U4, U18, and U25. I could not detect the number of the fourth craft. They were of a uniform size and U18 had painted on the conning-tower a huge Iron Cross, showing that it had achieved some great distinction—great, at least, to the German mind.

Hiring a rowing boat, and wearing my fez, I discovered the base of the submarines on the afternoon of January 15th. It was cleverly hidden behind two big German liners in the Golden Horn, between the Marine Arsenal and Has Keiul, the little village that had been entirely destroyed by the powder explosion. By this time, if my informant were correct—and I have no reason to doubt the accuracy of his statements, for, like so many Germans, he told me a good deal more than he ought—the number of submarines has been increased to six; he himself had been concerned in putting them together at Trieste. As a matter of fact, soon after my arrival in England I read in different neutral as well as English newspapers that two more German submarines of small size had arrived in Constantinople from an Austrian port in the Adriatic.

The German submarine officers and crews to be met with in Constantinople are not at all of the swaggering Prussian type. They wear the usual German uniform, whereas their fellows of the *Goeben* and *Breslau*, which fly the Turkish flag, wear the fez. The so-called Turkish submarines do not exist save in the imagination of certain people whose interest it is to write about them. They are in reality German submarines flying the German naval flag. I have reason to believe also that there are very few Turkish aeroplanes or flying-men. An American newspaper suggested that it was possibly a Turkish submarine that sunk the *Persia*; but as there are no Turkish submarines, one of them could not possibly have been guilty of this crime against civilisation.

These smaller submarines must not be confused with U51, which, as the German newspapers have proudly described, made the great voyage from Kiel to Constantinople, either through the English Channel or by the northern passage round Scotland. This took place in the spring of 1915.

The U51 is a huge craft, painted a dark grey, its appearance being very suggestive of its sinister purpose. It has a big gun mounted on the forepart. The size of the craft astonished me when I saw it some days after its arrival at Constantinople, on my first visit, and I think it must be one of the largest afloat. Unfortunately, I was not allowed on board: there were limitations to the privileges that my papers were able to secure for me. Beside this leviathan the U4 and her sisters would look mere pigmies; but they are vicious little craft, hornets with sharp and painful stings.

Now that Weddigen has been killed, Captain von Hersing is the popular hero of the German submarine navy. He is the type of man that possesses a strong appeal for the English sportsman. He is of the Max Horton order, and it was he who sank the *Triumph* and the *Majestic*.

In Germany heroes are made on the slightest possible provocation and for very indifferent achievements; but Captain von Hersing certainly deserves his fame. He is modest, a rather rare quality in the present-day German.

The story of his feat, which he narrated to me during my first visit to Constantinople, has already been told time after time. As quietly as any Englishman would have done he described to me that wonderful voyage; how he picked up petrol in the Bay of Biscay at an exactly appointed time and place; how he passed by Gibraltar in broad daylight on the surface of the water; the agonies he suffered during the imprisonment of his boat for two hours in a British submarine net off Lemnos; how he eventually escaped with a damaged propeller, and arrived at Constantinople in the early days of May.

During the whole recital of his achievements the nearest thing to self-glorification that I was able to detect in his manner was a momentary flashing of the eye, which no one would deny even to Admiral Beatty himself. He was disinclined to discuss the war, and I remember that at the time I thought how correct this attitude was in an officer, and how different from many of his fellows of the land service, who will discuss nothing else.

He told me that he had spent a considerable time in England, and that he liked the English. The promptness with which he denied that it was his boat that had sunk the *Lusitania* left me in no doubt as to his view of that colossal outrage. In fact, I have heard from many sources that the German Navy regards this discreditable exploit as a blot upon its name. I talked to him many times at the Pera Club, where there were comparatively few Germans and plenty of food, the one fact probably explaining the other.

If all Germans were of the same type as the German naval officers and men, the word "Hun" would probably never have been applied; it certainly would not so aptly fit. In their franker moments these naval officers and men confess that they hate the horrible work they are obliged to do; but that they have no alternative but to carry out the orders received from Berlin. There are brutes among them, no doubt, but such German naval officers as I have met compare very favourably with their swaggering colleagues of the land service. German sailors are under no misapprehension as to the might and efficiency of the British Navy. It is not they who spread the tale of the British Fleet hiding in ports while German ships proudly sail the North Sea. It is not they who ask plaintively, "Will the British Fleet never come out?" They are practical men, and for the most part honest men, and they know that

Germany has it in her own hands to bring out the British Fleet in no uncertain manner.

The Germans are annoyed because the valuable ships of the British Navy do not parade up and down in the neighbourhood of Heligoland and Wilhelmshaven and allow themselves to be torpedoed by German submarines. The German idea of naval warfare is sometimes childish, but it belongs to the layman and not to the expert. "Our people started the war ten years too soon," was the remark that one German officer made to me.

It is not difficult to see that there is very little love lost between the German Army and the German Navy, which is scarcely to be wondered at. A very casual observer has only to contrast the characters of the two classes of men, as I saw them at the Pera Palace Hotel; the one swaggering and strutting about, grumbling at the lack of amusement, growling if the *Liebesgabe* (parcel) from Berlin, with its sausage (*leberwurst*) and the like, cigars, and *pâté de fois gras*, is a day late; the other quiet, well-mannered, accustomed to great hardship and danger from childhood, self-respecting and respecting others— the nearest approach to an English gentleman that the Germans are capable of producing. Not many naval officers hail from the Hun country of Prussia.

It is beyond question true that the sinking of the *Lusitania* is terribly unpopular in the German Navy, although the German people went hysterical with joy about it, and still regard it as one of the great German feats of the war.

The presence of German submarines at Constantinople is not altogether relished by the Turks. Each of the four submarines I saw had a gun on the forepart of the vessel; not a powerful weapon, it is true, but quite sufficient to instil terror into the inhabitants of the city, should they not behave themselves according to German ideas.

There is still some antagonism shown in Turkey towards the Germans, but, unfortunately, very little. The German sway is almost supreme, but for all that they take no risks. They are conscious of an undercurrent of distrust, and they never allow the Turk too much ammunition, lest it may be used against themselves. It is notorious that the shortage of ammunition in Gallipoli was due not entirely to German inability to convey it there, but rather to the fact that the master did not trust the servant. A well-munitioned Turkey would be a danger, and ill-munitioned Turkey is a safeguard.

A little incident which came to my knowledge shows that even now the Germans have to exercise tact in dealing with the Turks. At the Hotel Tokatlian, in Pera, there was a daily foregathering of all the German and Austrian newspaper representatives in the city. One day I heard them discussing the fate of one of their number, Dr. Ledera, of the *Berliner Tageblatt*.

I gathered that he had offended the Turks by describing how, owing to the state of the *Goeben* and their own shortage of big guns, they had removed two of the largest from that vessel and taken them down for use against the English at Gallipoli. This information, which I brought to this country as early as last June, officially stated in so important a newspaper, intimated to the Russians and the British that the *Goeben* was practically out of action. The Turks were greatly incensed, and promptly arrested Dr. Ledera. He was sent to an internment-camp in a distant part of Anatolia, where the conditions were far from luxurious. The German Ambassador, the late Baron von Wangenheim, had to exert the utmost possible pressure to secure the release of his indiscreet compatriot. After six weeks' imprisonment the erring correspondent was brought back to Constantinople, escorted over the frontier, and ordered never to return to Turkey. In spite of this, each day leaves the Turk more hopelessly under the yoke of his German master.

I have always had my own views about the German spy system in England. Of one thing I am certain, that it is thorough; but, as I have previously pointed out, it is not so perfect as so many people in this country are inclined to believe. The first essential for a travelling German or Austrian spy is to obtain by fair means or by foul a passport from a neutral country. Only with this can he hope to enter England, and return in safety. I encountered one of these spies, and the conversation I had with him is of considerable interest as throwing light on German methods. He was an Austrian, and we got into conversation during my journey from Vienna to the Swiss border. As we approached the frontier he made obvious efforts to discover my views and sympathies. I allowed him first to express his own, which were violently pro-German. Nevertheless, he said, "I have been among those *Schweinhunden* twice in the last six months." (The "Schweinhunden," by the way, were the English.) "Fortunately, I did not allow the grass to grow under my feet during my seven years' residence there, and I flatter myself I can speak English as an Englishman. Do you know any English?" he asked.

"A little," I replied, in order to draw him out. He then began to converse with me in that tongue, and he undoubtedly was justified in his boast that he could speak English perfectly. Furthermore, he looked a very excellent and presentable specimen of the Anglo-Saxon race, such as one sees any morning during the London season, before the war, of course, in Bond Street, Pall Mall or Piccadilly.

In order to obtain a false passport the travelling spy must get first a false birth certificate. This, of course, involves forgery, but it can be obtained with no very great difficulty and at a reasonable price by those who know where to seek it. In the early days of the war there was a regular trade in passports in several neutral countries, where they could be purchased for between £10 and £12. Those days are now passed, for the English Government has awakened to the grave danger arising from this commerce.

With a birth certificate, in conjunction with a letter from some commercial firm to the effect that the bearer or person referred to wishes to proceed to England on certain business, the obtaining of a passport is not so difficult as it might appear. The documents are presented at the Passport Office of a neutral country and the necessary passport obtained. The next step is to get it *visé'd* by the British Consul, who is not as often English as he should be. When he is of English nationality he is frequently too old to be alert and on the lookout for spies. Once the passport is *visé'd* the travelling spy of German or Austrian birth or interests arrives at Folkestone, Tilbury, Southampton, or some other port where there is no lack of strict scrutiny. Lately the investigations have been especially severe, but of what avail is this if the passports and business letters that accompany it are based upon a forged birth certificate?

Arrived in England, the travelling spy communicates with the resident spy, cautiously lest the resident spy is being watched. In all probability they meet at a large hotel, or at a railway station, nothing is written. If an appointment has to be made it is done over the telephone or by a message through a third party.

In the early days of the war spies were inclined to be careless, being so convinced of the obtuseness of the English officials. The result was that a number of them attended an exclusive little party which gathered at dawn in the Tower of London. The censorship of letters has doubtless checked written communication to a very great extent.

To check spying the greatest care should be exercised by the British consuls abroad; they should never, unless absolutely confident of the *bona fides* of the bearer, *visé* a passport, and, of course, unless they do so the passport is absolutely worthless. If necessary, the British Consul should have the assistance of a shrewd international detective from England with a knowledge of foreign languages, a man who is accustomed to appraising character and ferreting out information; it would be difficult for the applicant to smooth away his suspicion, a thing which is very easy with most consuls.

The statement of my Austrian acquaintance that he had been twice to England within a period of six months (and I have no reason to doubt his word) shows that even now there are very obvious imperfections in the system for keeping spies out of England. In offering my views it is not with any idea of teaching the authorities their business, but rather the hint of one who has come into touch with the spies themselves, and in the hope that my words may be of assistance. It must be remembered that the authorities at the ports of entry can judge only on the actual papers produced.

CHAPTER IX

"OUR KAISER IS HERE!"

Getting Out of Constantinople—I Become Suspicious—I Appeal to Halil Bey—A Gloomy Apartment—I Visit the Prefecture of Police—I Join a Military Train—Marvellous Engineering—A Subtle Device—The Kaiser at Nish—I See the Two Monarchs—A Remarkable Stroke of Luck—I am Invited to the Banquet—Fokker Aeroplanes.

Secret service work in German-governed countries demands astuteness, resource, and constant watchfulness over words and actions alike, and a good deal of "Damn the consequences." To be known within the German war zone as one connected with an English newspaper would naturally be fatal.

Getting into an enemy country in war time is always difficult; but getting out of it is frequently precarious. I began to fear that I was being watched in Constantinople. The German system of watching is simple and effective. If the suspect be of sufficient importance three or four detectives are told off to follow his movements continuously, but one at a time. He is, therefore, not likely to recognise his watcher as would be the case if one man only were detailed for the duty.

Intuitively I felt that the few very innocent and harmless, but to me very important, papers I had with me were being subjected to examination in my room at the hotel. As a precaution I rearranged them, carefully noting the order in which they lay. When next I returned to the hotel in the evening my suspicions were confirmed—my papers had obviously been disturbed. It might, of course, have been mere curiosity on the part of the Greek servants, but I remembered that these same servants work hand and glove with the police or military authorities. Accordingly, I determined to get away with all possible expedition.

At that time it was announced in the very attenuated Constantinople newspapers that the Kaiser was going to Belgrade. The movements of the German Emperor on the Continent are as much of a puzzle to his own people and his allies as they are to the subjects of the Entente Powers. There were in Constantinople, too, the same rumours as to his ill-health which had been spread throughout Europe. On the other hand, there was the definite statement that he was coming East. The desire to see him face to face, if possible, and also the wish to get out of Constantinople, set me to work planning how most speedily to effect my purpose.

I bethought myself of Halil Bey, the Foreign Minister, who had so kindly secured for me an interview with Enver Pasha. To my surprise the old man saw me at once. His is a very different reception-room from that of his colleague, Enver. Gloomy, miserable, without electric light or even an oil lamp, and lit only by candles, it was far from the sort of room that one would expect to be occupied by a Minister of Foreign Affairs. It was, however, another evidence of the good work of the Roumanians in cutting off the coal supply of Constantinople.

I explained to Halil that it was my great desire to do myself the honour of seeing, if possible, the All-Highest War Lord, and that I wished to leave Constantinople for Belgrade. Halil Bey, in common with every other Turk, was in high spirits over the Gallipoli evacuation, and after a little judicious flattery as to his enormous powers, I succeeded in obtaining a letter to the Prefect of Police at Stamboul, and in order that he should see me instantly Halil gave me his card, which is reproduced below.

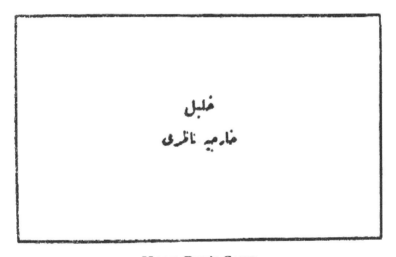

HALIL BEY'S CARD

I lost no time in securing one of the few public carriages that are to be had in the city, and made my way behind the thinnest pair of horses imaginable to the Prefecture of Police. It was rather like entering the lion's den, but it had to be done. If the police were really suspicious of me I should not be very long left in doubt.

I was a little disturbed to hear from the Prefect that the only way of getting out of Constantinople to Belgrade was by a German military train. The first Balkan Express which was to link up Constantinople with Berlin and Vienna, was not due to start for a day or two, and as I felt disinclined to wait for it, I determined to push on to Belgrade and join the Balkan Express there. This would give me a short time in which to examine that town, which, as I have said, I was most anxious to see. I mentioned to the Prefect that I had been honoured by Enver Pasha with an interview, and that I felt sure His Excellency would do anything in his power to facilitate my movements.

"I will see what can be done," said the Prefect. "Please leave with me your passport and call again in the morning."

With considerable trepidation I returned to the Prefecture next morning, and to my delight found my passport marked in Turkish not only with permission to leave, but with actual permission to travel by the military train to Belgrade. The "visieat" (a written permission from the police to leave), which usually takes a few days to obtain, was handed to me at the same time, so I was more favoured than any other traveller. I felt that the stars were indeed fighting for me in their courses. At 11.30 a.m. I arrived at the Railway Station at Stamboul, and soon found myself in a queerly assorted company consisting of men of the German Red Cross Service, German officers, non-commissioned officers and soldiers.

During my journey I made some curious and interesting discoveries, all tending to emphasise German thoroughness and cunning. Probably no one in England realises the wonderful work done by the Germans in repairing the broken railway bridges in Serbia. It is the rapid and substantial rebuilding of these bridges, destroyed by the Serbians in their retreat, that enables the Germans to get to Constantinople in a little over two days. These reconstructions are most likely the greatest engineering feats that the world has ever seen. Tunnels that were blown up have been restored to their original state with marvellous celerity, and as I travelled across the bridges, and at a high rate of speed, the evidences of the Serbians' tragic retreat were to be seen on every side. Beside the new bridges lay those which the Serbians destroyed. Beside the line were the remains of dead horses, broken-down carts, and the hundred and one things that mark the retreat of an army pursued by its foes. The ever-careful German had removed the hides from the horses, obviously with the object of making up the leather shortage.

In the course of my journey I received another instance of German forethought. I was told that in the event of Greece being invaded by the Bulgars, and the Greeks loathe the Bulgars as the Prussians loathe the English, the invaders were to be dressed in German uniforms in order to deceive the Greeks. Immense quantities of these uniforms, I later discovered, were lying at Nish.[1] Is there anything against which the extraordinary German mind does not provide? This, however, does not convince me that the Germans will attack Salonica. From what I heard, it would appear that they have a very wholesome respect for General Sarrail, whose acquaintance they had already made at Verdun, which they had failed to take owing to his able and stout defence of that stronghold.

The adaptability of the German is nowhere better emphasised than in Turkey and the Balkans. Instinctively he knows that a German in a familiar uniform is not likely to be so obnoxious as a German in a strange uniform; consequently his method is to disguise himself by adopting the military uniform of the country in which he is detailed for duty. This is one of the most important traits in his character. For instance, as I have already said, German flying-men in Turkey are to be seen in Turkish uniforms, and scores of German officers are to be found at the Turkish War Office also wearing the familiar uniform of the Moslem.

The Turks are by no means optimistic about the Salonica Expedition. Frankly they are afraid of it, and for that reason have heavily entrenched themselves to the south of Adrianople. Their fear is that the Allied troops may make an attack on Constantinople from the north-west or may attempt to cut the railway.

It has been suggested that my fortunate meeting with the Kaiser was a matter of luck. In a way it was; but it was more particularly due to my persistent desire to see Belgrade. I had failed to get there during my outward journey to Constantinople, but I was determined not to be baulked. I had no thought of staying at Nish, and it was not until we were approaching the station of that town that a fellow traveller, a German non-commissioned officer, looked out of the window and shouted out so loudly and excitedly that all the travellers in the corridor carriage could hear, "*Unser Kaiser ist hier*" (our Kaiser is here). I jumped up and looked out of the window and saw the flags and decorations, and felt that indeed Fate had been kind to me.

The magic name of the Kaiser was too much for me. I could not think of letting pass such a magnificent opportunity of seeing the Great War Lord, and I therefore determined to leave the military train at the Serbian town so recently the capital, but now in the hands of the Germans. Nish was under snow. The day of my arrival, January 18th, 1916, was brilliantly clear, just such a day as one finds at Montreal or St. Moritz. I had hoped to get at least a glimpse of the Kaiser, but I was far more fortunate than that, encountering him on several occasions during this to me fateful day. I never for one moment anticipated being present at that curious and historical Royal Banquet at which were made the vain-glorious Latin and German speeches that were telegraphed all over the world.

Just as our train steamed into the station the Kaiser was making his state entry into the Serbian capital, which has now become the headquarters of the German, not as many people think the Austrian, Army in the Balkans. It is a vast arsenal, choked with munitions of war, in particular shells for big guns and also the guns themselves. The town is crammed with Serbian military prisoners, who are allowed their liberty, and roam about freely. They seem comparatively contented with their lot.

My feelings when I ascertained the presence of the Kaiser can only be appreciated or understood by a journalist. I soon gathered together my belongings with the aid of a German soldier I called to help me. I then decided to look around and endeavour to approach as near as possible to the Kaiser himself. As a matter of fact I was not far away from him. King Ferdinand had only a few minutes previously received him on his arrival from the West, and the Royal pair were walking up and down the platform arm in arm, and without ceremony. I noticed a handkerchief in the Kaiser's hand which he was constantly lifting to his mouth, but the distance was too great for me to hear him coughing.

I had never seen Ferdinand before, and it was fully eight years since I had seen the German Emperor, and what a change those eight years had wrought! The Kaiser is not a tall man, as he is represented to be in photographs, and by the side of the great massive figure of the hawk-nosed Ferdinand—who has a duck-like waddle—the Great War Lord seemed almost diminutive. The Kaiser wore a long grey coat, with greyish fur collar, and a spiked helmet covered with some khaki-like material. The place where the monarchs promenaded was held by German guards. The people, among whom were a great many Austrian and a few Dutch nurses, did not evince a great amount of either interest or curiosity. This struck me as strange as, if the Kaiser were to appear in any other town in Europe, he would create a sensation. I particularly noticed that the Bulgarian Ministers obsequiously removed their hats at the sight of the Kaiser, and approached him in an attitude of great deference and with bared heads. Towards their own monarch they did not seem to show the same deference. Later I learned that the relations between Ferdinand and his Court are of a very informal nature.

What most struck me about the Kaiser was his obvious look of fatigue. It might have been due to the war, to the effect of his two-day journey, or to ill-health. I cannot say. But he looked a tired and broken man. His hair was white, although his moustache was still suspiciously dark, and his face was drawn and lined. There was also an entire absence of the old activity of gesture, the quick, nervous wheeling about, and the unstable manner of the man. All of which I remembered distinctly from my previous encounter with him in 1908.

In spite, however, of his fatigues the Kaiser was obviously intent upon making himself agreeable. He examined with apparent interest the medals of the Bulgarian soldiers, chatting with Royal affability, and smiled right and left. None the less he was a greatly aged man, and, as I have said, there was the constant use of the handkerchief, a large Turkish affair of red, embroidered with the white Turkish star and crescent in the corner.

As I was standing watching the Royal pair, I was approached by two Bulgarian officials in civil clothes followed by a handful of soldiers. Their mission was to inquire my reason for coming to Nish. The one who addressed me spoke German execrably. At first he took me for a Teuton, but when I explained my nationality he asked eagerly if I were able to speak French, and seemed much delighted when he found he could continue his interrogations in that tongue, which he spoke much better than German. I told him the object of my journey, flattered his patriotic feelings by complimenting the Bulgarian Army and nation as a whole, and was invited to accompany him to one of the rooms of the station, where he introduced me to the Chief of the Bulgarian Press Bureau, M. Romakoff. I seemed to have made a good impression on the two Bulgarian officials. They babbled away in their native tongue to M. Romakoff, but, of course, I could not understand what they were saying, but the upshot of the conversation was that I was addressed by the Chief of the Press Bureau, and asked if I would like on behalf of the neutral press to attend the Royal Banquet, which was to be given that evening. It would be simple but historic. I trembled with excitement and joy when I thought of the sensation that my account of the banquet would make when it reached England. If M. Romakoff could have read my thoughts it would not have been the banquet alone about which I trembled, but my own execution; fortunately he was not psychic.

The Director walked with me up and down the platform and showed himself extremely friendly. I gathered that I should be one of four journalists in the room, and I hugged myself at the thought of the surprise of the august company when they realised that in their midst was the representative of a hated English newspaper.

I spent the intervening time between my arrival at Nish and the hour of the banquet in walking about the town with two members of the Bulgarian Press Bureau, who spoke excellent French. I had no idea what impression they gleaned as to my personality. I must be a clever actor to have disguised my excitement into even reasonable coherence.

But a few weeks previously Nish had been gaily decorated with the flags of the Entente Allies, who were expected to come to the help of poor, suffering Serbia; yet the town seemed already to have settled down to a comparatively contented existence. Very little damage had been done to any of the buildings, as far as I could discover. I was assured that business had not been so brisk during the whole of the history of the town. German soldiers were spending their money freely, and nearly all the larger houses of the town had been turned into hospitals, whose supplies were being gathered from the surrounding country.

As we strolled about I noticed the departure of the Royal train and the arrival of a munition train, including several trucks laden with Fokker monoplanes. I do not claim to any special knowledge of aeroplanes, but these new Fokkers struck me as having a very great wing expanse. For the purpose of railway transport the wings were fastened back and the engines carefully covered. A Fokker monoplane is so long that it occupies practically the whole of two large trucks.

FOOTNOTE:

[1] As I correct the proofs, February 15th, I read on the authority of the *Morning Post's* Athens correspondent, that some time ago three of the best Bulgarian divisions on the Doiran front were withdrawn to Sofia, where they were clothed as Germans, afterwards returning to their stations!

CHAPTER X

THE BANQUET AT NISH

> The Banqueting Hall—A Small Gathering—The Menu—
> The Kaiser and King Ferdinand—Von Falkenhayn—An
> Impressive Figure—The Kaiser's Health—His Poor
> Appetite—Constant Coughing—King Ferdinand's
> Triumph—The Bulgarian Princes—German Journalism—
> A Bombastic Oration—"Hail, Cæsar!"—The Kaiser's
> Unspoken Reply—The Hour of "The Fox"—The End of
> an Historic Function—The Post Office Closed.

The Banquet was held in the Town Hall of Nish. The banqueting-room was profusely decorated with the flags and the colours of the Germanic Powers, although Austria is not in great evidence at Nish, having apparently made Belgrade her headquarters. When I entered the room I was surprised to find that the function was to be a comparatively small one. There were not more than fifty covers, and several of the places were empty, the actual attendance being about forty. The band of the Life Guards, numbering about twenty, was ensconced behind palms, and played a programme of music which is here reproduced.

```
                                    Leib-Garde-Regiment



              Musik-Programm
           für die Königliche Mittagstafel
                  am 18. Januar 1916.


        1. Polonaise, . . . . . . . . . . . . . Bubeck
        2. Ruy Blas — Ouverture . . . . . . . . Mendelsohn
        3. „Hussarenwalzer" . . . . . . . . . . Ziehrer
        4. „Tannhäuser" Fantasie. . . . . . . . Wagner
        5. „Die Zauber-Quelle" . . . . . . . . . Atanassow
        6. „Zigeunerfest". . . . . . . . . . . . Lehar
        7. „Meistersinger" Potpourri . . . . . . Wagner
        8. „Valse brillante" . . . . . . . . . . Chopin
        9. „Der fliegende Holländer" . . . . . . Wagner
       10. Balkanmarsch . . . . . . . . . . . . Skordew
```

PROGRAMME OF MUSIC AT THE NISH BANQUET

There were three tables, forming three sides of a square; or perhaps it would be more accurate to say, parallelogram. They were simply decorated with roses and early spring flowers, yellow being the predominating colour. The Banquet, of which simplicity was the predominating feature, was served by Bulgarian soldier servants. The menu card is reproduced here, and I append a translation.

MENU AT THE NISH BANQUET

THE KAISER'S MENU.

BALKAN DISHES.

[*Translation.*]

NISH, JANUARY 18, 1916.

ROYAL DINNER.

The coat of arms at the top is the Bulgarian Royal Arms of King Ferdinand. It is embossed in the original in black, red, and gold. One of the chains round the crest is probably that of the Golden Fleece.

The dishes are as follow:

>Chicken broth.
>Trout from Lake Ochrida (west of Monastir).
>Pilaff of lamb.
>(Pilaff is a Balkan stew, with rice.)
>Venison à la Cumberland.
>(The Duke now with the enemy.)
>Pâté de foie gras.
>Fennel from Varna (Bulgaria) and endive.
>(Fennel is a reedy vegetable used in salad
>or cooked with butter.)
>Bulgarian ice.
>Cheese straws.
>Dessert.

As might be expected from the German military authorities, their arrangements for the Press were excellent. Our seats were close to the Royal party, and we had no difficulty in hearing the speeches.

The Nish banquet was of the usual Royal stiffness. I should probably have remarked many more things, but for my excitement and nervousness. The Kaiser sat on King Ferdinand's right, and on King Ferdinand's left sat General von Falkenhayn, the chief of the German General Staff, whilst M. Radoslavoff, the Bulgarian premier, was placed on the right of the Kaiser. Interested as I was in the Kaiser, I was hardly less interested in the personality of von Falkenhayn, who is the brain of the great German War Machine. Although a man well into the fifties, he looks as if he had not yet crossed the half-century mark. It would be difficult to find a man with more refined and good-looking features. There is nothing markedly German about him, except perhaps his thoroughness, and I obtained the impression that the Germans have in him a war director of remarkable ability. He is trim and alert of movement, has close-cropped grey hair, and seems the personification of vigour, virility, and vivacity. He appears to be bearing the strain of war and its tremendous responsibilities in a remarkable manner. Seldom have I met a man who has struck me as being so well-fitted for the work before him as von Falkenhayn. Whenever I looked across at him as he sat chatting quite freely with the Kaiser and Ferdinand, I had the impression that here was a man with far-reaching vision and great executive power.

I sat less than fifteen yards away from the Royal pair, and I had every chance of observing closely each change in expression or smile that flitted across their countenances. Now as I look back on the scene I see the Kaiser, not only perpetually coughing, but also looking so tired that I wonder afresh what great purpose it was that brought him from a sick-bed in Berlin to a little

Serbian town with its dim petroleum lamps. It must have been something unusually important that caused him to accept the Little Czar's invitation to travel for two days to be a guest at a dinner of forty covers. Whatever the Kaiser's sufferings he was obviously endeavouring to be as pleasant as possible.

Everything I remember in connection with the Banquet confirms me in my impression that the War Lord was deliberately intent, not only on impressing King Ferdinand, but the members of his entourage as well, otherwise he could never have tolerated the air of equality which the Coburger adopted towards him. The Kaiser is by nature intolerant of patronage or condescension on the part even of his equals, much less would he view unmoved that of an inferior unless he had some deliberate purpose in view. He looked a pathetic figure as he sat coughing, as though his throat were choked with some virulent, irritating substance, and it must have cost him a great effort to smile repeatedly as Ferdinand leaned across and whispered something in his ear.

I found myself speculating as to what was passing through the Kaiser's brain as he saw the yellow face, with its cunning little slits of eyes—eyes that reminded me of a typical money-lender—of his vain-glorious neighbour bent upon him. Try as he will, Ferdinand of Bulgaria can never disguise the suggestion of craftiness that is stamped upon his features. Those little eyes of his seem to be the windows of a very dark soul, and behind that pepper and salt-bearded face, with the great hawk-like nose, there is a very cunning brain at work. From the fact that the Kaiser ate and drank practically nothing at the Banquet I was led to believe the story that he always eats before attending these State functions. Of course, it might have been that he was afraid of his throat. Certainly monarch never did less justice to an admirably-cooked meal. He did not even take wine. On the other hand, Ferdinand ate of each and all the dishes with great appetite, sipping his special brand of white wine with evident relish. Of all the company he seemed best pleased with himself, and when I noticed him studying the menu, it occurred to me that his vanity was flattered by seeing at the top his own Royal Cypher; it was his, Ferdinand of Bulgaria's Banquet, and the All-Highest had journeyed for two long days and nights in order to be present.

I was glad that the Bulgar King was in a good humour, because when he smiles the grossness of his features is less obvious. The contrast between the Emperor and King was most marked, however, when they stood up.

By the side of the big, clumsy-looking Ferdinand the Kaiser appeared almost insignificant, but it was not his size that so engrossed my attention. All through the meal I could scarcely take my eyes from the haggard face of the author of the world-war who, on this January afternoon, looked so little like a war lord, as he sat apparently coughing away his life into the Turkish woven handkerchief which he held firmly in his right hand. His hair was terribly white, darkening a little at the parting where the roots showed. His cheeks were scored with many lines, and when I conjured up the vision of the healthy-looking Kaiser I had seen eight years previously in Amsterdam, I could not help marvelling at the change that those eight years had wrought in him. The only thing about him that was not changed was his upright deportment. He stood up firm and erect, just as one had seen him taking the salute at manœuvres or when reviewing his Prussian Guard. His pose was that of an Emperor, and contrasted strangely with the heavy awkwardness of his brother monarch.

Among the other guests present were the two young Bulgarian princes. The Crown Prince Boris must have been a terrible disappointment to his father. He is round-shouldered and thin, and might, were he not a prince, have been aptly described as a lout. I do not think I am prejudiced in saying that but for his clothes he might as well have been a menial employed in his own father's household. His expression entirely lacked intelligence, and he looked much older than his years. Perhaps the failings of his father, which he has possibly inherited, may account for this worn-out appearance. He gave me the impression of one greatly fatigued. He is far from handsome, with the big Coburg nose, but fortunately not constructed on so large a scale as that of his father. Prince Cyril, the younger brother, unlike Prince Boris, is of a much better appearance, and seems more intelligent, but of neither has their father any reason to be excessively proud. Both the young princes sat between German officers, and having once been acknowledged by the Kaiser, seemed to relapse into the insignificance for which they were so pre-eminently fitted by nature.

Perhaps one of the most amusing things in connection with the Banquet at Nish was the report of a German paper that the Kaiser, who was in joyous and playful mood, picked up Prince Cyril, tossed him up into the air, and placed him on his Royal knee and kissed him. In the enthusiasm of the moment the German journalist must have forgotten the Kaiser's withered arm, which would have rendered it impossible for him, however playful his mood, to "toss" an infant of a week old. Furthermore, as I have explained, Prince Cyril is a young man fully-grown, and of far too loutish and uninteresting an appearance to invite the kisses even of the diplomatic Kaiser. However much that august monarch might have desired to propitiate the Bulgarian King, he would certainly have stopped short of kissing Prince Cyril. Sometimes German journalists over-reach themselves.

The speeches, which were political and bombastic in character, were fully reported everywhere a few days after the Banquet. They were not, as has been stated in some quarters, delivered in English. King Ferdinand's grandiloquent address to the Kaiser was, with the exception of the Latin phrases, delivered exclusively in German, excellent German by the way. The Bulgarian monarch spoke easily and without notes. He seemed to experience no difficulty in finding words. I did not take down the speeches, I confess that I was far too excited for that, besides I knew that they would be distributed throughout the civilized world through the agency of the German Press Bureau. I have referred to the columns of *The Times* in order to refresh my memory.

We were engaged with Bismarck cigars and coffee when there was a sudden hush in the hum of conversation. The hour of the speeches had arrived. There was a tense excitement as King Ferdinand rose. He did so with the air of a man who was conscious that he had reached the one great moment of his life. His voice was clearly heard in all parts of the room, and his delivery was extremely good. He began by pointing out that two hundred and fifteen years ago that day Frederick the First was crowned King, and forty-five years ago the New Germany was founded. To-day the Kaiser, after the glorious victory which had attended his arms, could with safety enter the former Roman fortress of Nish. King Ferdinand tendered his thanks to the Kaiser for his visit to the ancient town, a visit which cemented the alliance between the two countries.

"The world," he contended, "has learnt to appreciate with surprise and admiration the strength of Germany and her allies, and believes in the invincibility of the German Army under the guidance and leadership of its Kaiser."

The King expressed the hope that 1916 might bring "lasting peace, the sacred fruits of our victories, a peace which will allow my people to co-operate in future in the work of Kultur, but, if fate should impose upon us a continuation of the war, then my people in arms will be ready to do its duty to the last."

At this point King Ferdinand apparently found German entirely inadequate to the proper expression of his feelings, and that nothing short of a classical tongue would suffice.

"Ave! Imperator, Cæsar et Rex," he burst forth, "Victor et gloriosus es. Nissa antiqua omnes Orientis populi te salutant redemptorem, ferentem oppressis prosperitatem atque salutem. Long live Kaiser Wilhelm!"

[*Translation.*]

"Hail! Emperor, Cæsar and King. Thou art victor and glorious. In ancient Nish all the peoples of the East salute thee, the redeemer, bringing to the oppressed prosperity and salvation."

All this to a man who was bearing the strain of the occasion with obvious effort. Even whilst listening to the sonorous periods that proclaimed him Cæsar and a number of other things, he coughed into that handkerchief with its stars and crescent.

The Kaiser's official reply, which by the way was never spoken, but was disseminated by order of the authorities, ran as follows:—

"Your Majesty has especially dwelt to-day on the three important epochs which coincide with this day. Very often as a young man, at the side of my grandfather, and later as ruler, I have celebrated this memorable day, always of the same importance, surrounded by the Knights of the Order.

"Now for the second time, by God's decision, I celebrate it in the field, on old historic ground, a beautiful piece of country conquered by Bulgarian bravery, received by the King amidst his brave troops and their illustrious leaders and honoured by your Majesty with a high order, but above all with the appointment of Colonel of the 12th Balkan Infantry Regiment. Thus your Majesty has done me an honour than which I could expect no better.

"To-day you have given me the fulfilment of a long cherished wish, and your words prove that we, in valuing this hour, are filled with the same feelings. We have been challenged by our enemies, who envied Germany and Austria-Hungary their peaceful and flourishing prosperity, and in most light-hearted manner endangered the development of the Kultur of the whole of Europe, in order to strike us and our loyal allies at the root of our strength.

"We have had a hard fight, which will soon spread further.

"When Turkey was threatened by the same enemies, she joined us and in stubborn fighting secured her world position.

"Your Majesty's prudence recognised that the hour had come for Bulgaria, for you, to bring forward your old and good claims and smooth the way for your brave country to a glorious future. In true comradeship the glorious triumphal march of your Majesty's nation in arms began, which, under the guidance of its illustrious War Lord, has added one sublime leaf of glory to another in the history of Bulgaria.

"In order to give visible expression to my feelings for such deeds, and to the feelings of all Germany, I have begged your Majesty to accept the dignity of Prussian Field-Marshal, and I am, with my Army, happy that you, by accepting it, also in this sense, have become one of us.

"With God's gracious help great deeds have been accomplished here and on all other fronts.

"I experience feelings of the deepest gratitude to the Almighty that it has to-day been granted me, on this historic spot, once more consecrated with brave blood, amidst our victorious troops, to press your Majesty's hands and listen to your Majesty's words, in which is manifest the firm determination to fight for a successful and lasting peace, and to continue the loyalty and friendship sealed in the storm of war, in true common labour for the high task imposed upon us by care for the welfare of our peoples.

"With the firmest confidence I also pursue this aim, and raise my glass to the welfare of your Majesty and your House, to the victory of the glorious Bulgarian army and to Bulgaria's future."[2]

The dinner was held on the two hundred and fifteenth anniversary of the coronation of Frederick the First, and the founding by him of the order of the Black Eagle. It is this fact that the Kaiser refers to in the first paragraph of his reply.

As a matter of fact, the only other speaker at the Banquet in addition to King Ferdinand was Von Falkenhayn. He rose to respond briefly to a few compliments that Ferdinand had bestowed upon him. One thing is certain, that the Kaiser could not, had he wished, have delivered his oration on account of the incessant cough which troubled him throughout the evening.

At the close of the Banquet, which was as excellently served as it had been well-cooked, the German and Bulgarian National Anthems were played, and the historic function, which throughout had been of an extreme simplicity, broke up with an informality that in itself was distinctive. Here were some of the great actors in the greatest drama of the world's history performing, not for the benefit of the worthy citizens of the equally worthy little Serbian town of Nish, but for the people of the whole civilised world. My last impression of the two chief characters was that of Ferdinand, with a cunning gleam in his little slits of eyes, clasping the Kaiser's right hand in both of his own. Was it to cement some important pledge, or was it merely warmth of feeling on the part of him who had earned the name of "The Fox" I wonder!

Immediately I left the Town Hall I dashed off in company with the other journalists to the post office, in the hope of being able to get my narrative off to London *via* the neutral country to which I belong; but I had reckoned without the German press censors, who no doubt inspired their Bulgarian brethren to close the telegraph office so that nothing should leave Nish without first having been submitted to the Bureau. But I felt that my news would wait, and I determined to catch the Balkan Express to Vienna.

Since my return to England I have received many messages full of the kindest congratulations upon my account of the Banquet at Nish. I do not wish to pose as a hero who does not understand the meaning of fear. Not even the

Kaiser himself was more uncomfortable than I. What I ate I do not know. I suppose I did eat. I was fully conscious that were I recognised by one of the numerous Secret Service officers about the Kaiser, or by any other person who had happened to see me during one of my previous visits, either to Germany or the Near East, there would have been a short and simple ceremony by the wall of the Town Hall, in which a firing party and myself would have been the protagonists.

As I left the Banqueting Hall I felt as Alexander must have felt at the thought of there being no more countries to conquer. I had achieved, by a wonderful combination of circumstances, what I had never dreamed of achieving, and now all I desired was to get back to England to tell the whole story. I began to be in terror of discovery; such a trick on the part of Fate would be a supreme effort of irony. Only one thing remained for me to do, and that was to get back with the utmost possible expedition, but as it turned out I had yet other experiences. I was to travel to Vienna by the famous Balkan Express, the "Balkan-Zug," as it is known to the Germans, which connects Berlin and Vienna with Constantinople.

FOOTNOTE:

[2] The author's acknowledgments are due to the editor of *The Times*, from which the speeches are quoted, and to Reuter's Agency for permission to quote the Kaiser's reply.

CHAPTER XI

THE BALKAN EXPRESS

> Existence of the Balkan-Zug Denied—A Great Strategical Factor—The Publicity Train—German Economy—I Join the Balkan-Zug at Nish—King Ferdinand a Fellow-Passenger—His Condescension—Excellent Food—Ruined Belgrade—Arrival at Buda Pesth—A Tremendous Ovation—Russian Prisoners at Work—Arrival at Vienna—Another Tremendous Reception—Remarkable Punctuality.

I have seen it stated in *Le Temps* that the Balkan Express does not exist, that it is a bluff on the part of the Germans. I really cannot understand how a responsible editor of an influential paper can make such an assertion without first ascertaining whether or no he be writing the truth. Does he realise that he is misleading the people, which is calculated to do very serious harm to the cause of the Allies? The importance of the existence of this Balkan Express cannot be exaggerated, and its usefulness should not be under-estimated.

First of all, the Balkan Express *does* exist, as I have travelled by it myself. It is one of the most perfectly-organised railway services I have ever seen, and I have seen many. This service enables the Germans to transfer all sorts of *matériel* to and from Berlin to Constantinople, and is therefore one of a series of great factors in the present war. By its aid German troops can be rushed to Constantinople within 56 hours, and from there transferred to whatever front most needs them.

It took me five days to travel from Vienna to Constantinople, along a miserable route, changing trains frequently. On my return journey I entered my compartment in the train at Nish and never left it until I reached my destination, Vienna, and that within 40 hours.

The Germans themselves are by no means eager that their foes should appreciate the great value, to them, of the Balkan Express. If the Allies can be made to believe that it does not exist they will in consequence become re-assured as to German plans in the Near East, and thus unconsciously aid those same plans by not being in a position to upset them. The Germans have great ambitions as regards, not only the Near East but the Far East also, and much of their energy is at present concentrated upon the realisation of those ambitions in Turkey, the Balkans, and Asia Minor. "To Egypt!" is something more than a mere political cry.

The Germans have strength, resources, and a grim determination to materialise those ambitions which shall strike at the power of the hated English in what they conceive to be its most vulnerable point, the Suez Canal. Nothing would please them better than, by virtue of misrepresentation of the true situation in the countries of the Entente Powers, that they should be enabled to spring a great and dramatic surprise upon their enemies. That is why I write feelingly about the statement to which I refer above. The Balkan Express will in all probability become one of the great factors in the situation in the Near East. It must be remembered that it is something more than a train for the conveyance of passengers. It will become in all probability of great strategical importance. I had seen it suggested in British as well as foreign newspapers that the Balkan-Constantinople Railway is not working properly; the following account, I think, will be something of a revelation to many of the doubters.

The Balkan Express is the show train of the world. Never has there been a train with such grave responsibilities. It might well be called "the Publicity Train," for its object at present is to advertise German victory and German thoroughness. Later it has sterner work to do. It is probably the handsomest train in Europe, and beyond doubt has been designed by the Germans with the object of impressing the thousands of people of various nationalities who gaze on it in wonder twice a week on its way from Berlin to Constantinople and twice a week from Constantinople to Berlin. The admiration of the Turks is tempered with alarm, for the Turk is no fool, and he sees that the efficiency which has enabled the Germans to reach Turkey may be the very barrier that hinders them from ever leaving it.

The Balkan-Zug, as it is called in the Central Empires, is, however, a source of unqualified delight to Germans, Austrians, Hungarians, Bulgarians, and the rest of the people who see it on its journey. Its name is blazoned in three-foot letters on each wagon. Engine and carriages are decorated with flags and flowers, and every passenger wears in his buttonhole a German flag on which appear the words "Balkan-Zug" and the date.

I had originally intended to join the Balkan Express at Constantinople, but as it would not be starting for two or three days I had booked my place upon it, securing my ticket at Constantinople, with the intention of boarding it at Belgrade, but circumstances had decided otherwise. When purchasing my ticket I had an illustration of the seriousness of the money question in Constantinople. Eight months previously when I was there gold was given at the banks in return for cheques, that, however, had developed into a shortage not only of gold but of silver, as I have explained, and for my ticket which really cost 870 piastres (£8), I had to pay the equivalent of £12 about, owing to the decrease in value of the Turkish £.

MY TICKET FOR THE FIRST BALKAN EXPRESS TO RUN FROM CONSTANTINOPLE TO BERLIN AND VIENNA

My ticket for the Balkan Express, the outside of which is reproduced here, is an illustration of German economy and also of German fallibility. Surely a nation that is spending millions of money each day to achieve its object could have afforded the few hundred marks required for printing a special ticket for the Balkan-Zug. The tickets are the old sleeping-car tickets in German, with the words "Balkan-Express" printed across in English. Possibly this is due to a breakdown on the part of the printer entrusted with the preparation of the new ticket, but it would certainly have been more in keeping with German methods had there been prepared not only an elaborate ticket but a souvenir of the journey. It must be remembered that this was the first journey of the Balkan Express west, that is, from Constantinople to Berlin, and consequently it was historic.

After the Banquet I strolled about the town, then going to the railway station gathered together my possessions and waited. The Balkan-Zug was late. Night was upon us before it drew into Nish station, an impressive affair consisting of four sleeping cars, one dining-car, and one ordinary first and second class car. As it steamed into the station the German, Bulgarian, and Austrian National Anthems were played, and King Ferdinand and his two unprepossessing sons entered before the rest of the passengers. This was an interesting event also for the passengers from Constantinople, who leaned out of the windows, keenly interested.

The Kaiser had disappeared immediately after the Banquet, just as the Kaiser always does disappear, suddenly and mysteriously, no one knowing why or whither. Unceremoniously his Bulgarian Majesty climbed into the train, and we, the smaller fry, followed after him, I feeling rather like the camel of whom it is said that his supercilious air is the outcome of knowing the hundredth great secret of the Universe, whereas man knows only ninety-nine.

In the course of the evening King Ferdinand, without ceremony, entered all the compartments in the train and made a few general remarks to each person separately. He seemed desirous of displaying his Royal person. He was a king and a factor in the great political situation, and he seemed equally determined that no one on the Balkan-Zug should be allowed to remain in ignorance of that very important fact.

In the carriage next to mine there was traveling the Baroness von Wangenheim, the widow of the late German Ambassador at Constantinople, and with her were her three little daughters, whom Ferdinand took on his knees and fondled. It was obvious that he was mightily pleased with himself. When he waddled into my compartment we rose, clicked heels, and bowed. He graciously gave us the Royal consent to be seated, and spoke a few words to a Hungarian, who was one of the party, in his own tongue. This man afterwards told me that the King spoke the Hungarian language like a native. It is well known that Ferdinand is an excellent linguist. The other passengers in my compartment were two German flying-men in Turkish uniforms, who with ten others that were in the train had been suddenly recalled from Constantinople to take part, it was said, in forthcoming air raids on England. These raids, by the way, duly took place, and according to German official accounts reduced industrial England to a pile of ruins!

King Ferdinand adopts quite the Kaiser's method of speech. He accepts the Almighty as an ally. "Thanks to God," he said, "Who greatly helped us we can travel from West to East through conquered territory in a few days. We are going further. Give my Royal salute to all the people of your home country." He then withdrew, and we permitted ourselves to relax our spines.

On the Balkan Express the food is infinitely better than can be obtained in Constantinople, Vienna, or Berlin. It may almost be said of the Germans that they have one eye on God and the other eye on advertisement in case of accidents. I felt convinced that the food on the Balkan Express was superior merely for advertising purposes. Bread-tickets are unknown, and for a mark I had an early breakfast of coffee, rolls, butter and marmalade without stint.

It was about ten o'clock at night when we reached Belgrade, which, as I have said, I was particularly anxious to see. On inquiry I found that the Balkan Express was to remain there for an hour and a half, and, determined not to be disappointed, I left the station to stroll around the town, or rather the ruins of the town.

Some idea of the accuracy of modern artillery fire may be gleaned from the fact that the besieging Austrian gunners were able to aim with such precision that not one shell had fallen on the railway station. It must be remembered that they were firing from the other side of the Danube at its widest part. The Austrian Staff had obviously realised that their advancing army would have need of the railway as soon as the Serbians had been forced back, and doubtless the artillery had been instructed at all costs to spare this important point. The remarkable thing, however, is that houses within a few yards of the station itself have been absolutely destroyed, yet there was not so much as a mark that I was able to see upon any of the station buildings themselves.

The Kaiser had already been in Belgrade, and the German Wireless Agency took occasion to inform the world at large that "Since the days of Barbarossa, who on a crusade to the Holy Land held a review of over 100,000 German Knights in Belgrade, no German Emperor has set foot on Belgrade's citadel until that day, when the German Emperor arrived in splendid weather and was greeted by an Austro-Hungarian guard of honour and military music, shouting, and the roar of cannon.

"The Emperor visited the new railway bridge, and then went amongst the festively-clad population, who freely moved about, and afterwards rode to Kalimegdan, the excursion resort. The Emperor afterwards held a review of the German troops, which crossed the Danube, and addressed them with a speech thanking them, and felicitating them on their extraordinary exploits. The Kaiser personally delivered Iron Crosses to the soldiers."

To me it seemed only a few days before that Belgrade had fallen into the hands of the Huns, yet already the river was spanned by a wonderful new wooden bridge, such as could not be constructed in a few weeks, or months, for that matter. In all probability this and many other bridges had been built years back in preparation for the great struggle that Germany and Austria alone knew was impending. This was no temporary makeshift, but as good as the fine American trestle-bridges in use on the best American railways.

The Germans seemed to be prepared for everything; in particular are they prepared against England, their most hated foe. I wish that I could get Englishmen to ponder over this, to them, vital fact. Had there been an invasion of England, a thing which now fortunately seems impossible, the truth would have been brought home to that country with tragic suddenness. Germans were not only ready for war, but as the war progresses they are ceaselessly improving their *matériel*. Everywhere I went I saw evidences of this.

As I returned to the station, having just seen the terrible fate that had overtaken the Serbian capital, I could not help wondering why it is that England seems incapable of appreciating her danger. I refer, of course, to the population in general, for many of those in high places, I am convinced, have no illusions as to the political and strategical situation.

I had been somewhat surprised to find that the Balkan-Zug had not received its usual enthusiastic reception at Belgrade. Possibly this may have been because of the late hour of its arrival, but more likely because the civil population of the town has practically ceased to exist. Belgrade is now the Austrian main headquarters on that front, and is essentially a military town.

We drew out of the station shortly before midnight, and arrived at Buda Pesth between nine and ten o'clock the next morning. In the Hungarian capital the Publicity Train received a tremendous reception—ovation would be a better word. At the Nord Bahnhof there was an enormous crowd, the greatest I have ever seen at a railway station. The excitable Hungarians tumbled over each other in their anxiety to get near the Zug. Wine was brought for the engine driver and fireman, and the passengers, with their little Balkan-Zug flags in their coat buttonholes, were promptly lionised, and—for once in their lives at least—experienced the sensation of being popular heroes. The crowd patted them on the back, insisted on shaking hands with them, cooed over them, crowed over them, and laughed with hysterical joy. What pleasure can possibly accrue to a man leaning out of a railway-carriage window from shaking hands with entire strangers, I cannot possibly conceive; yet it seemed to give intense satisfaction alike to the passengers and the populace.

At Buda Pesth the Balkan-Zug was tidied and made presentable. Windows were cleaned by men having little ladders, and the compartments and corridors swept. To my great surprise I found that this work was being done by big, bearded men in Russian uniforms. I spoke to one or two of them, but they had very few words of German. They explained that they were Russian prisoners. I was surprised that they had with them no guards of any description, and appeared to be without supervision. I commented on the fact to a fellow passenger, the Hungarian I mentioned before, who told me that the men were left entirely to themselves, and that they were too content with their lot to wish to make any endeavour to escape. He said they were kindly treated, and always expressed their satisfaction at being where they were, and much preferred it to returning to Russia to fight. I was under no illusion on this score, however. A Russian private soldier is not such a fool as to imagine that he stands the least possible chance of escape from an enemy country when he has at his command only a few words of the language in use in that country. Probably the Russians found that the best way to ensure good treatment was to simulate entire content.

Advertising by train is nothing particularly new. I have seen it done in Canada and the United States of America; but advertising victory by train is about the most convincing method of spreading the splendid news that I have ever encountered. Everybody who has seen the Balkan-Zug will tell everybody else that they have done so, not once, but many times. These persons in turn will tell others, embroidering the story somewhat, and so the ball will go on for ever rolling. The Balkan-Zug is photographed and described in countless journals, and it appears on myriads of post-cards. I have never seen such enthusiasm in England except in connection with some famous football player, the idol of a crowd numbering fifty or sixty thousand persons. It would be invidious to draw a comparison between German and English methods in this respect.

At Buda Pesth the Publicity Train divided itself into two parts. Another beflagged locomotive appeared, like a bridegroom seeking his bride: in this case it was only half a bride. One half of the train goes to Berlin and the other half to Vienna. As it was my object to get to England as speedily as possible, in order to give my account of the Kaiser's health and King Ferdinand's famous Banquet to *The Daily Mail*, I determined to go to Vienna. I was one of the very few of the passengers going to the Austrian capital. The officers and the flying men proceeded to Berlin. Those of us who had come from Constantinople were looking forward to somewhat improved food, which we hoped to obtain in Vienna. As yet the newly-opened line to Constantinople has had time merely to take the Balkan-Zug and the military trains carrying army supplies, men, and munitions for the Baghdad, the Caucasus, or the Egyptian ventures, possibly for all. My last glimpse of the Berlin half of the Balkan-Zug was of the still hysterical mass of people endeavouring to buy the little flags worn by the passengers. Later, in Vienna, I was offered 20 kronen (about 16s.) for mine, but I refused it. Subsequently I was offered a much larger sum.

During the journey to Vienna I talked with a Turkish gentleman and his wife and daughter. I was greatly amused to hear that, although the women had left Constantinople veiled and dressed in Eastern costume, as soon as they crossed the border both put on European clothes and dropped the veil. They expressed the opinion that now the Germans had opened up Turkey with the famous railway, the state of semi-starvation in Constantinople would cease. Personally, I had doubts, which I tactfully refrained from expressing.

I had seen Germany in war time and been in several of its principal towns, and I knew that, whatever the German newspapers may tell to the world, there is no surplus food in any part of the country that I had visited. The old Turkish gentleman was shrewd and kindly, and he expressed his regret at the closing of all the French schools in Constantinople. He volunteered the information that, in order that his son should not absorb the principles of German militarism, he had sent him to be educated at a school in French Switzerland.

Vienna gave the train what the newspapers call a rousing reception. Even the official mind gave way before it, and the Custom House officers and other functionaries spared us the usual examination and interrogation. Not even our passports were examined. I came to the conclusion that there was great virtue in being a traveller by the first Balkan-Zug running from Constantinople to Vienna. Knowing, however, the ways of the military authorities in the war zone, and that later on I should be obliged to prove my arrival in Vienna, I insisted on having my papers stamped by the military authorities at the railway station.

At Vienna tickets were collected from the passengers as they left the station. I had determined to make a great effort to retain mine, of all my papers the most important next to my passport. As I was about to pass through the barrier, an official held out his hand for my ticket. I explained to him that as I had been a passenger on the Balkan Express I was anxious for sentimental reasons to retain it. I gilded my remarks with a tip of five kronen, which seemed to satisfy him, as he very kindly tore off a portion of the ticket and returned to me the remainder. But for this official venality I should not have been able to reproduce this valuable evidence in this volume.

My journey from Vienna to Constantinople by way of Bucharest had occupied five days. The opening of the direct Vienna-Constantinople line reduces this to two nights and two days—50 hours, to be exact. Even now the train arrives at the various stations with remarkable punctuality, always within five minutes of the scheduled time, which in itself is a triumph for German organisation.

CHAPTER XII

FRENCH THOROUGHNESS

I Leave Vienna—I am Ordered Back—I Risk Proceeding on My Journey—A Friendly Hungarian Officer—Over the Swiss Frontier—My Frankness My Undoing—The French Super-Official—I am Detained Somewhere in France—My Protests Unavailing—I am Suspected of the Plague—Left Behind—*The Daily Mail* to the Rescue—Profuse Apologies—I Proceed to Paris—"You Will Never Convince England"—London at Last—Rest.

I had only four hours in Vienna, and in that time there was a great deal to do, which I had better not detail here lest I get someone into trouble. The train for Feldkirch, the station on the Austrian-Swiss frontier from which I had set out a few weeks previously, was just on the point of starting when I climbed into the carriage, my hand luggage being bundled in behind me.

I was beginning to breathe more freely now that I was on my way to a neutral country. At the end of about an hour, when I really felt justified in congratulating myself upon being practically safe, an official came through to my compartment of the train, asking to see the passport of each passenger. He examined mine with that slow and irritating deliberation peculiar to these officials, and, looking up suddenly, said:

"This has not been signed by the police."

"What police?" I inquired.

"The police of Vienna," he responded.

"Surely that is not necessary," I remarked. "I only arrived by the Balkan Express at three o'clock, and had my passport stamped at the station." It will be remembered that I had insisted upon this being done, foreseeing possible difficulties.

"I am afraid," he said, "that you will have to get out at the next station and go back." He was extremely polite, but very firm.

I said that I was just returning from a most important visit, and showed him the document which I had obtained at the War Office (the Kriegsministerium Pressbureau) in Vienna, and which had already many times saved the situation.

"Well, if you can satisfy the frontier authorities," he replied, "I have nothing to say."

I became very uneasy, but I decided to proceed. It would indeed be an irony if I were to be discovered within hail of safety. I slept very little that night, and when we arrived at Feldkirch, on the following afternoon, I braced myself up for a final struggle with the authorities. I looked about me anxiously to see if the official whom I had encountered in the train had come on to Feldkirch, and I was greatly relieved that he was nowhere to be seen.

We were all ushered into a large waiting-room, the same waiting-room that I had entered a few weeks previously when setting out on my journey. One by one the other passengers were admitted to the adjoining room, just as they had been admitted previously, and at the same table were to be seen five military officers, smoking, and sitting in judgment. As I entered the room I felt like a prisoner going up the steps to the dock at the Old Bailey to receive sentence.

However, the good fortune that has attended me throughout my journey did not desert me at the last moment, for my examining officer was a very nice young Hungarian, who was so interested in the narrative of my journey, and what I had seen in Constantinople, that he subjected my papers to a very cursory examination. The papers themselves were, thanks to my careful precautions, in perfect order save for the absence of the ridiculous and unnecessary superscription by the police at Vienna. This young officer then accompanied me to the train, gave me his card, and asked me to look him up next time I was in Buda Pesth. Needless to say I shall not do so, but he was not in the least to blame for passing me through. The worst he could have done would have been to send me back to Vienna that my passport might be signed by the police, and my friend the Hofrat would have seen that no difficulty would be allowed to arise in that direction.

Once over the frontier at Buchs in Switzerland, I breathed as a prisoner might be expected to breathe on regaining his freedom. For seven weeks I had been in constant danger of discovery, and during that time I had been forced to act and dissimulate, and for ever watch myself and others lest some chance remark of mine might arouse suspicion in the minds of those about me. The mental strain had been tremendous, and this had reacted upon the body, for during those seven weeks I lost more than a stone in weight.

I do not think that I am a coward, at least not a greater coward than the average man, but I was greatly delighted to find myself safe once more. No one who has not been through such an experience as mine can understand the feeling of elation and delight that comes with the knowledge that at last he is absolutely a free man.

My journey from Constantinople to Switzerland had probably established a record, at least since the beginning of the war; but, alas! my future progress was not to be so rapid. The officials at the French frontier were far more exacting than those of the enemy country through which I had passed, and I cheerfully tender this tribute as to their efficiency, although at the same time I should like them to know that they caused me considerable inconvenience. At Berne I had to wait four hours for the train, which no longer goes direct to Paris, the passengers having to change at Pontarlier. On the previous occasion when I had travelled by that route the train had travelled direct from Berne to Paris. The reason for this change I discovered was that it had been found that spies secreted documents in the carriages before being personally examined, and when they were "passed" they recovered their missing papers and continued the journey with the documents upon them. Accordingly the authorities very wisely so arranged it that passengers had to change trains at Pontarlier on the Swiss-French frontier. It will be seen that cleverness and subtlety are not the monopoly of the Germans.

At one time Pontarlier looked like being the Waterloo of my little trip. By certain means—which it is not my intention to disclose—I had placed myself in a position that I could verify every stage of my journey by documents, which I intended to produce should the Germans deny the veracity of my statements, or should my truthfulness be questioned in other quarters. Knowing the Germans as I do, I am convinced that Dr. Hammann, the head of the German Press Bureau, would adopt one of two courses. He would either forbid the publication in the German newspapers of a single word of my story, or he would frankly challenge its accuracy. Apparently he has chosen the former course, as not a word about it has appeared in any German paper, or Austrian, for that matter, most of which I see. The German accounts of the Banquet at Nish represent the Kaiser as in a merry mood. What a travesty of truth!

As I was now in France, and conscious of my own sympathies with the Allies, I thought that there would be no harm in disclosing the whole of my documents. Accordingly when my turn came to be examined by the *commissaire*, I said straight out that I had come from Constantinople. Instead of being hailed as a hero, I was given to understand, albeit politely, that in all probability I had adopted this course of showing all my papers because I was not merely a spy, but a super-spy, who had conceived the brilliant idea that the best plan of getting past the French authorities was to affect an attitude of colossal candour. In vain I protested and expostulated. In vain I pointed out that it was essential that I should arrive in London with the utmost possible expedition. I suggested that if they distrusted me they could send with me an official, every official they possessed for that matter, whose expenses I would pay to Paris, where they could easily satisfy themselves at the Paris office of *The Daily Mail* that I was what I represented myself to be. Talk of German thoroughness, German caution, and German patriotism! The Germans have much to learn from those excessively courteous but severe French officials, who cannot be won over by the flattery which goes so far in Germany. If the official I had encountered thought that I was a super-spy, I am convinced that he was a super-official. Now that it is all over I have for him nothing but admiration, but at the time his persistent courtesy made me feel that I should like to hit him.

Nothing would satisfy him but that I should be stripped, and this fact he conveyed to me in the most courteous phraseology, at which I suggested with some acerbity that he would still be courteous even were he leading me to the guillotine! None the less, stripped I had to be.

My collection of papers, which has proved a source of such interest to so many distinguished and highly placed people in this country, was minutely examined, and certain maps and other important documents, whose interest is rather military than journalistic, were temporarily taken from me. I was in a panic of anxiety. The minutes were passing, and the time for the Paris train to start was drawing near. I implored the authorities to telephone to Paris, and then it was that they played their trump card. They intimated that seeing I had come through Austria, and understanding that the Plague was prevalent in Hungary, they felt obliged to detain me for medical examination next morning. It was then midnight. Neither my expostulations nor my entreaties produced the least effect upon the impassively polite Frenchman. I verily believe that had there been no Plague in Hungary as an excuse for my detention, that they would have had me examined for foot-and-mouth disease, glanders, or rinderpest. One of the most anguishing moments of my life was when I heard the Paris express slowly moving out of the station. I, of all the passengers, being the only one left behind, and I of all the passengers the one in the greatest hurry to get to Paris.

Soon philosophy came to my aid, and I argued that how like life it was. After the many risks that I had run in enemy countries, where I had never been even detained by the officials, here was I, immediately on getting to what should have been friendly soil, being examined and cross-examined and re-examined again and again by officials whose every word spoke suspicion. I had been equal to every previous examination to which I had been subjected, and here was I stranded at the very moment of success in the country of one of the Allies for whom I had so great an admiration. "*Gott im Himmel!*" I muttered, "spare me from my friends."

Within a few minutes of the departure of the train there came a reply by telephone from Paris guaranteeing my integrity, accompanied by a request that every possible facility should be given to me. This produced an official *volte face*. The courtesy remained the same, but there were full and adequate apologies. The French authorities seemed genuinely distressed at the inconvenience they had caused me. Indeed, nothing could be more kindly and courteous than the treatment I received at Pontarlier. In spite of the delay that these men had caused me, I respected them for their thoroughness. It is better in war time to err, if error there must be, on the side of caution.

I doubt if I could have written these friendly words at the time. I was feeling too irritated to recognise virtue in anyone, least of all in a French official. There was no train until five o'clock the next afternoon, and that, I was informed, was an omnibus train, stopping at every station between Pontarlier and Dijon.

By taking it rather than wait for the later express, I was informed, I should save two hours on the road to Paris. The Hotel de la Poste, at Pontarlier, had long since been asleep, but I aroused it, delighted at the opportunity of myself being able to inconvenience somebody else, and I spent a wretched night of chagrin and worry. Would there be further difficulties? Should I ever get to London? Should I for any possible reason be detained in Paris? It must be remembered that I had a great story burning in my brain. None but a journalist can understand that instinct which prompts a man who has obtained "good copy" to dash for the nearest point where that copy can be turned into print.

Only those who have moved about in war time with documents and maps in their possession have the least conception of the difficulties that arise with the authorities, who naturally have every reason to be suspicious.

It was at three o'clock in the afternoon on January 25th, exactly a week after the historic Banquet at Nish, that I reached London, and without a pause proceeded to the offices of *The Daily Mail*, where I had scarcely sufficient strength to write the account of my meeting with the Kaiser at Nish. I then made for my hotel, enjoyed a luxurious bath, and a long, long sleep. I was utterly exhausted.

It must be remembered that I had been travelling continuously for a week, that is, from the evening of the Banquet at Nish, January 18th, until three o'clock on the afternoon of the 25th. In Serbia and Austria all the sleeping-cars had been requisitioned by the authorities, which added greatly to the fatigues of travel; but I had the satisfaction of knowing that I had carried out my instructions, and had brought back what I had been told to bring back— a living story.

I have had the satisfaction of opening the eyes of the British public to the strange migration of Germans to the Near East. I can tell them with a conviction, that with me is almost passionate, that unless the Allies obtain a smashing victory, the German occupation of Asia Minor will threaten England's hold on India, England's hold on Egypt, the Russian security in the Caucasus, and will open up to Germany a vast granary that will completely destroy the effect of the British Blockade and alter the whole history of the world. I am not an alarmist, I am a journalist who has seen many strange things, things which no other man of either a neutral or Entente Power has seen, and being a journalist I understand to some extent the relation of cause and effect. "You will never convince England of her danger," someone recently remarked to me. "But why?" I asked; "what possible object can I have in exaggerating or lying? I am not a politician, I am not even an Englishman, and certainly I feel very deeply the danger the Entente cause is running, owing to the spell of apathy that seems to have fallen upon certain sections of the public." My friend's reply was a smile.

It has been a great pleasure to me, too, to be the instrument of showing how a highly organised newspaper can act as an effective means of obtaining information for a nation at war. The police of this country have long since recognised the value of the Press in detecting crime, and I think the Government will now have an equal respect for the journalist as a secret service agent, albeit an honorary one. I know of at least one newspaper that has a most wonderful organisation in the enemy countries for securing information, and that organisation is not excelled by any Government of the Entente Powers.

One word of warning to British officials at present occupying posts as Consuls and Ministers. They must appreciate the fact that this war concerns their country's very existence, and they must not allow themselves to be lulled to a false security by mendacious statements that appear in the press. One distinguished English diplomatist in a neutral country, a man whose name is well known in the diplomatic world, said to me only a few weeks ago, "And do those silly Germans really think they are going to win?" and his remark was accompanied by a superior and incredulous smile.

"Why, of course, they do," I replied, "and unless England wakes up perhaps they will." I felt annoyed with the man.

CHAPTER XIII

THE GERMAN MENACE

>After Thoughts—The Great Factor—National Service—False Ideals as to the German Soldier—The Danger of Under-estimating Germany's Resources—Great Britain's Helpers—Crush the German—"Wait Till We Get to England."

Now that I am back in London quietly meditating on my recent experiences, I cannot help feeling ill at ease. I see in my mind's eye once more, just as if I were sitting at a kinematograph show, those thousands of young, sturdy-looking Germans on their way to the Near East. I see the magnificent new bridges and the reconstructed tunnels in Serbia. I hear the crowds at different stations cheer the Balkan Express on its way back to Berlin. "Are people in this country," I ask myself, "fully aware of the seriousness of the present situation? Does the Government of this country fully realise that unless the British Fleet be left to show its might in cutting off what is the food of the German War-Machine, the war itself cannot be brought to a successful issue?"

Great changes have taken place since I left London at the beginning of November. On my return I find that National Service has been adopted by the Government and accepted by the people. To me this was the best news I had heard for many months. A step nearer victory, I told myself.

At last the British people have realised that compulsion to defend the country of their birth is no disgrace, and they have learned that it in no way threatens their personal liberty. The French and Dutch, to mention two countries famed for their love of independence and liberty, never have and never will consider it against their freedom to be compelled to learn how to defend themselves in the hour of need. An Englishman does not consider it a disgrace to be compelled to pay his rates and taxes; why should it be regarded as anything but an honour, and a very great honour, to be compelled to defend the greatest freedom that subjects of any country have ever known—to give up his life for his Motherland?

The adoption of the National Service Scheme has caused me the liveliest possible satisfaction, but there is still another danger to be met by, not only the British people, but the British Government itself; that is, the under-estimation of the power and resources of the German menace. The misleading statements which for the past year have figured in many English journals, to the effect that men of fifty and boys of fifteen are sent to the front on account of the exhaustion of German man power, have done incalculable harm in convincing thousands of people that the end of the war is at hand, and that the end will be victory for the Entente Powers. The Germans have now been fighting for eighteen months, and they are very far from being beaten.

A man may, to his own entire satisfaction, come to the conclusion that given the Spring and sufficient munitions that the German resistance will crumble. The German resistance will never crumble; it will fight as fine a defensive campaign as it has fought a series of offensive campaigns. To under-rate an enemy is to undermine your own chances of victory.

Shortly after my return to England I was talking with a Frenchman who for some time has lived in this country. He seemed to be convinced that the Germans had only old men and boys in the trenches in France, and that they were a mere army of cowards.

"If that be the case," I replied, "if they really are an army of cowards who throw down their arms and hold up their hands as soon as they are attacked, then why does not the glorious French Army hurl them back across the Rhine?"

To this my friend made no reply. I relate the incident merely to show how many excellent people hypnotise themselves into the belief that the Germans are cowards. Any British "Tommy" who has participated in an attack on the German trenches, or who has helped to hold the lines against a German onslaught, will confirm me in my opinion that the Germans are very far indeed from being cowards.

It will aid the Allies nothing to underestimate German cunning and German efficiency. I firmly believe that in the long run Great Britain can hold out far better than her foes; but Great Britain is not fighting alone, she has to consider France, Russia and Italy, and finish this fight with the utmost possible expedition.

It is incumbent upon this country to put forth its entire manhood, as well as to husband all its resources for the great struggle that is looming in the very near distance. In short, all must wake up to the great German danger. Away with kid gloves! Away with all thought of the Hague Convention! Fight the reckless, ferocious, wild animal which has broken loose over Europe, fight it with every weapon at your disposal! If Great Britain allows this animal to conquer it, there will be no pity, and the glorious British Empire will be a thing of the past. Those thousands and thousands of young men of the Empire from every corner of the globe who have died on the battlefields of France and Gallipoli shall then not have died in vain, and the most glorious monument to the memory of those fallen heroes will be the complete defeat of the brutal Hun.

This is not the hour for seeking personal glory, but it is the moment for searching for efficiency, be it in the field of battle or on the Government benches in the House of Commons.

Britons, as well as neutrals, who love this, to me, dear old country and all that it stands for should give their all to crush Germany. The blunders that have been made are for the most part almost excusable blunders. No one can expect that in a short time a country that has always been anti-militarist can turn into a highly organised military power. The Germans themselves have taken some forty years to achieve this. I repeat, Germany is still very far from being beaten. Personally I firmly believe in the eventual victory of the Allies, but only if every man according to his ability throws the weight of his influence, his money, or his life into the scale. Then, and then only, shall we see the German War Machine break down, one part after another, and once more peace shall be restored to a Europe torn with strife and soaked with blood.

France, Russia and Italy are merely Great Britain's helpers. Great Britain is the real opponent to German Militarism. She is the great store-house from which supplies and munitions pour, and without which her Allies cannot continue the struggle. It is she who is fated to be the great factor in the crushing of German ambition, and its mad lust for world-wide domination. Germany is to this century what Napoleon was to the last, a menace to individual and national independence. It has been seen what German Kultur did for Belgium and Serbia. "Wait till we get to England!" is a remark I have heard from German lips, uttered in a tone so significant, so sinister, that I have involuntarily shuddered.

Milton Keynes UK
Ingram Content Group UK Ltd.
UKHW012314040624
443649UK00007B/622